A Kramsky Scrap Book.

A biography of Kramsky, Wales.

As collated by Robert Barth from 1988-2019.

ISBN 978-1-78222-860-8

Book design, layout and production management by Into Print
www.intoprint.net
+44 (0)1604 832149

A Kramsky Scrap Book

Robert was born in May 1971 in Wimbledon and was brought up in Surrey. He was a modest person known for his gentle nature, great sense of humour and he was always full of surprises. He had a gift for mathematics from an early age, also languages, photography and music. He won a photography competition as a young boy and passed the musical Bentley test as well as teaching himself piano. He married Francesca, who is Italian, in 2003, and quickly learnt the language. He loved nature and animals especially cats, of which they had five.

He was an avid reader always learning and recently wrote articles for the *Pioneer* and in the *Swansea History Journal*. Genealogy research was his great love, spending his spare time between running his computer business and renovating their house, researching into his family and their origins and also working on his ever-growing family tree from the age of 15.

Hence this book.

Jack Kramsky – his maternal great grandfather – held a special fascination for him; from his escape from Russia as a 13-year-old stowaway on a ship ending up in South Wales and not America, his intended destination with dreams of a better life. Jack was a kind religious man and a real character, confirmed by his many run-ins with the law while bringing up his large family.

In the Scrap Book, there is plenty of information on Swansea and the Gower coast which held special memories for Robert. Two years ago on a trip to Swansea he managed to retrace many of the journeys made by Jack.

At the age of 17 Robert persuaded his maternal grandmother Esther, who was brought up in Wales, and his grandfather Freddy, an escapee from Germany, to tell their life stories into a tape recorder. Which tales Robert then typed up into booklets, some of which are included in this book along with other family anecdotes and extracts.

Dedication

Sadly Robert passed away at the age 49 from Covid in February 2021 before quite completing his book but there is plenty of research here on the Kramsky family and Swansea.

This book is dedicated to Robert's memory.

Robert with Sheila and Rita outside 154 Bishopston Road – on a trip down memory lane.

CONTENTS

1. Coming to "America"

Unknown Kramsky kids, in Russia, around 1900

Jack Kramsky

Jack Kramsky was born on 1st December 1886, in Pechera, a small town roughly between Kiev and Odessa, in the Podolia guberniya. It was then part of the sprawling Russian Empire, and is nowadays situated in the Vinnytsia oblast of western Ukraine.

He was the first child of Solomon & Bashi Kramsky, recent immigrants from Poland. In the 1880s, the population of the Podolia was 12% Jewish, being as it was right in the middle of the "Pale of Settlement", a region covering roughly modern-day Latvia, Lithuania, Poland, Belarus, Moldova, Ukraine, Crimea and parts of Russia.

The Jewish population of Podolia had exploded in the 1850s-1870s, rising to nearly half a million. After the introduction of the restrictive anti-Jewish "May Laws" of 1882, which were tightened after 1892, and due to frequent outbreaks of pogroms which left hundreds killed, many Jews emigrated to the USA, Argentina or Palestine. More than two million Jews had left the Russian Empire by 1920.

In around the year 1900, attracted by dreams of a better life in America, so the story goes, Jack stowed away on a ship with his friend, both of them aged 13. When discovered, they avoided being put ashore by helping the crew paint the ship; the fact that Jack was a good singer also endeared him to the captain. When they were put off at the next port, they found themselves not in America, but in Plymouth.

Looking hungrily into a grocer's shop window, a voice asked them "Du bis jiddische boys?" and offered them to "Kommen haym mit me, and have a Shabbes meal." After looking after the boys for a few days, it turned out that this man had a widowed sister who lived in the Welsh valleys, in the coal-mining town of Penrhiwceiber. She needed help with her house, her three children, and her drapery shop, and Jack was the right man for the job. His friend joined the army, pretending to be much older; two years later Jack had to pay to get him out.

After a couple of years saving his shillings, often carrying the children to school on his back, and earning money wherever he could, including working a rollerball game at the local fairground, Jack could afford to take over the woman's shop.

Крамско́й

On Jack's 1924 passport, his name is written in Cyrillic script:

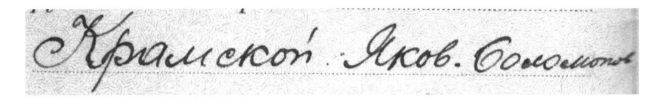

Крамской Яаков соломоново

This transliterates as KRAMSKY, JACOV SOLOMONICH, i.e. Kramsky, Jacob, son of Solomon.

The Cyrillic alphabet is used (with local variations) in Russia, Ukraine, Belarus, and other Slavic and Turkic countries.

Surnames ending –ski and –sky are common in most Slavic countries, such as Poland, Russia, and Ukraine. The feminine ending, used by all women, is -ska or –skaya, who would have been known as "**Kramska**" or "**Kramskaya**"

This name has been converted into English in different ways over the centuries. There is no right or wrong way of converting between alphabets, only conventions and local customs. For example we can find other families called Kramski in Poland & Germany, Kramskoy & Kramskaya in Russia & Ukraine, and Kramskoi & Kramskiy in Russia. Our own spelling of Kramsky is now found primarily in Mexico & the USA, much more so than in Eastern Europe!

Exactly what is meant by "Kram" is open to interpretation. Possibilities include :

- Shop - from Kram in Polish, or крама in Belarusian
- Crimea - from Крим in Ukrainian, or Крым in Russian - i.e. Krym
- Variations of various towns or areas in Poland, Belarus, etc.

2. Penrhiwceiber and beyond

Penrhiwceiber Road in about 1910.
Maybe there's a Kramsky in there somewhere?

Penrhiwceiber

Penrhiwceiber, a small town in the steep Cynon Valley in South Wales, was virtually non-existent until coal was discovered there. The "Penrikyber Colliery" was constructed in 1878, and employed up to 2000 men at its peak in the 1920s. After the 1940s the colliery went into decline, and ultimately closed down in 1985.

The Jewish population seems to have been only 2 or 3 families, with slightly larger populations in nearby Pontypridd and Aberdare. On the whole Jews were tolerated as friends and neighbours, and were often defended from the more extremist views, such as those that led to the anti-Jewish rioting in Tredegar in 1911.

Trading as a painter, plumber and glazier, in clothes and furniture, Jack certainly had an interesting time in Penrhiwceiber, appearing in the local newspapers at least 20 times, winning and losing his legal battles in equal measure, including bankruptcy in 1909, before moving the family out of town in 1913.

Newspaper clippings & business info (over the next few pages) :

1907

• "J Kromsky, painters & plumbers, Penrhiwceiber Road." Paying £22 annual rent. • Jack is at the Jewish Ball in Aberdare; • Gives fishknives as a wedding present.

1908

• "Kramsky, 185a Pen. Road." • Jack is at the Jewish Ball again; • Sues the Great Western Railway for damaging a shipment of Belgian glass panes worth £1.14s;

• Trousers worth 17s stolen from his shop door; • £18 of clothes stolen; Solomon knocked down but kept hold of parcels; men sentenced to 12 months' hard labour.

1909

• A horse hired to carry some furniture knocked a man down, and no one was sure who to sue (not Jack of course); • Solomon (glazier) & Jacob (furniture) taken to court for illegally selling some hired furniture; • Jack's business seems to have gone bankrupt.

1910

• "Trades / Outfitters, 30 Pen. Road" AND "Plumbers & Glaziers, 161 Pen. Road" • Sued for a "loan" of £5 from Solomon, by a man who caught a train. • "Samuel A Krawsky, general dealer at 214 Pen. Road"

1913

• Sued someone for not paying for some glass, while moving out of town.

SOUTH WALES

AND

MONMOUTHSHIRE

DIRECTORY

AND

BUYERS' GUIDE,

1907.

Printers and Publishers:

E. F. COPE & CO.,

STANDARD WORKS, WALSALL;

The Aberdare Leader

March 9, 1907

PENRHIWCEIBER

AND

MOUNTAIN ASH.

Sale of Valuable Leasehold and
Freehold Properties.

MR. JAMES H. JAMES (of the
firm of Messrs. Morgan and
James) has received instructions to Sell
by Public Auction at the Bailey's Arms,
Miskin, Mountain Ash, on

TUESDAY, MARCH 12th, 1907,

at 7.30 p.m. (subject to such conditions
of sale as shall be produced and read at
the time of sale), the following

PROPERTIES.

LOT 5.—All that shop, dwelling-house
and premises situate in Penrhiwceiber
Road, on the Tyrarlwyd Estate, now in
the occupation of Mr. Kransky, at the
gross annual rental of £22 10s. A lease
of these premises will be granted to the
purchaser for a term of 99 years from
the 1st day of January, 1900, at the
yearly ground rent of £3.

The Aberdare Leader

February 22, 1908

Mountain Ash County Court.

TUESDAY.—Before His Honour Judge
J. Bryn Roberts.

BROKEN GLASS. — Jacob Kransky,
185a, Penrhiwceiber-road, represented
by Mr. S. Shipton, sued the G.W.R.
Co. for £1 14s. damages for glass broken
in transit from Bristol to Mountain
Ash. Plaintiff said that 17 sheets of
glass had broken, and he charged 2s. per
sheet.—In reply to the Solicitor for the
G.W.R., Kransky said that the glass was
made in Belgium, from which place it
was consigned to Bristol.—Robert Og-
borne, an employee of the Bristol firm
which supplied Kransky with glass,
said that the glass was not broken when
forwarded from Bristol. — Thos. Gwat-
kin, station-master G.W.R. Mountain
Ash, said that with regard to 7 sheets
the notice sent in by plaintiff came too
late.—His Honour then gave judgment
for 34s. less the 14s.

May 9, 1908

Mountain Ash Police Court.

THURSDAY (to-day). — Before Sir T. Marchant Williams (Stipendiary), Major Morgan. Capt. G. A. Evans, Ald. D. Prosser.

THEFT.—E. J. Woodman and Frank Floyd, Penrhiwceiber, were brought up for stealing three pairs of trousers, value 17s., from the shop door of Jacob Kransky.—Woodman, one of the prisoners, said they only took two pairs.—L. Levinson, pawnbroker, said that on May 5th Woodman pledged one pair in his shop. He advanced 2s. on it. Next day Floyd pledged the other pair.—P.C. Bennett deposed to arresting prisoners. Woodman said to him: "I own I took one trousers," and Floyd said. "One pair I had."—Both prisoners pleaded guilty, and they were sentenced to prison for 14 days.

EVENING EXPRESS AND EVENING MAIL,

MARCH 25, 1909.

KNOCKED DOWN BY RUNAWAY

A case of peculiar interest was heard at Mountain Ash County-court on Wednesday (before his Honour Judge Bryn Roberts). Edward Brown, of Penrhiwceiber, claimed damages for injuries done to him by a runaway horse at Miskin, Mountain Ash, on April 4, 1908. Plaintiff was in a doubt as to whom he should claim from, since the runaway horse belonged to one defendant, was hired from that defendant by another defendant, but at the time of the accident was in charge of no one. The animal really belonged to John Gough, grocer, from whom Jacob Kranski, furniture dealer, had hired the horse and cart.—His Honour thought it was a matter of business.—Judgment was granted to plaintiff, who was represented by Mr. William Kenshole, with damages at £10, defendant Gough to pay all costs.

Struggle for Parcels.

Mountain Ash Burglary Charge.

At Mountain Ash Police Court on Thursday before Sir T. Marchant Williams, Col. Morgan and Capt. G. Evans. Benjamin Levinson, shop assistant, (who was defended by Mr Gwilym Jones), Price Lloyd, shop assistant, David Lloyd, his brother, and William Bryant, a brother-in-law, colliers, were brought up in custody charged with burglariously entering a shop in Penrhiwceiber-road, Mountain Ash, and stealing wearing apparel, of the estimated value of £18 17s 6d, the property of Jacob Kramsky. Mr W. Thomas, solicitor, Aberdare, defended the three last-named defendants.

Jacob Kramsky said his shop was broken into on the night of the 10th inst. and the goods (produced) stolen.

Minnie Kramsky, a sister of prosecutor said that on Sunday afternoon, she saw Levinson and Price Lloyd carrying parcels from Pengeulan Cottage. She told her father, who sent her brother for the police. Levinson was approached by her father, and they struggled for the parcels. Levinson knocked her father down and then went back to Pengeulan Cottage.

Solomon Kramsky said he took hold of Levinson and said, "I think you are carrying my son's goods and I want to get them.' Levinson replied, " These are your son's goods, but I have bought them, and will not give them back. Leave me alone." Witness said, " Kill me if you like, but I will get my son's goods." He managed to keep the parcels.

P.C. George said that on Monday, 16th inst., he was in the Police Station when Levinson was brought in. He was searched, and a number of skeleton keys (produced) were found on him, also a knuckleduster. On the 18th inst. he went to Kramsky's shop and found that the biggest key would open the shop door.

P.C. Richard Thomas said that on Sunday last David Lloyd was in custody in witness's charge. He remarked to witness, " I am in a mess now, but I know nothing at all about it. I happened to be in the house when the stuff was brought there."

P.S. Bolton, Miskin, said that on Sunday night last he visited 4, Pengeulan Cottages, in the occupation of William Bryant. David Lloyd lived in apartments there. Under the roof he found two parcels containing wearing apparel, which he now produced, and Mrs Bryant identified the apron containing the parcels as hers. He subsequently arrested William Bryant. He charged David Lloyd and Bryant on Sunday night, and both said they knew nothing of it. On Monday morning he visited the shop which Benjamin Levinson managed, in company with his father, and found the three parcels (produced) behind the counter. Levinson was then charged, and replied, " Not guilty." Price Lloyd also said, " Not guilty." Cross-examined by Mr W. Thomas: He knew Price Lloyd and B. Levinson were friendly. He knew Lloyd travelled for drapery, and was in the habit of taking parcels of drapery into Bryant's house. He had ascertained that Bryant was working the night of the burglary.

David Lloyd and Bryant were committed for trial in their own recognisances, but the Bench declined to accept bail for the other two, who were removed in custody.

PENRHIWCEIBER.

Kramsky Solomon, glazier, 161 Penrhiwceiber road
Kramsky Solomon, outfitter, 30 Penrhiwceiber road

[KELLY'S

Kelly's Directory 1910

EVENING EXPRESS AND EVENING MAIL.
THURSDAY, FEBRUARY 10, 1910.

"BY TRAIN FOR A WALK."

A singular transaction was disclosed at Pontypridd County-court to-day before Judge Bryn Roberts, when Morris Sunshine, Treforest, claimed £5 from Solomon Kramsky, Penrhiwceiber, alleged to be money lent. Mr. Crockett was for the plaintiff, and Mr. D. Rees (Messrs. W. R. Davies and Co.) defended. Plaintiff averred that Kramsky, who was a stranger to him, asked for the loan of £5 to pay off his son's creditors. A brother-in-law, T. Andrews, was present when the money was paid over by cheque. Andrews in the witness-box caused some amusement when he informed the court that he had gone to Treforest "by train for a walk." He denied that he owed Kransky £5 4s. for goods supplied. His wife might have had them. Mr. Rees submitted that the money given to Kransky was in payment of the amount due from Andrews, who was the real borrower, Sunshine having security from him in goods removed from his shop to Treforest when he retired from business at Penrhiwceiber. Judgment for defendant.

The Aberdare Leader

January 18, 1913

"Call Probert First!"

Jacob Kramsky, Penrhiwceiber, sued David Hann, 214 Penrhiwceiber Road, for 20s. 9d., for goods supplied. Plaintiff sold defendant some glass. Defendant paid him 20s. on account, leaving a balance of 20s. 9d.

Defendant was conducting his own case, and denied owing any money, having paid all but 9d. to plaintiff, this amount being paid into court. Defendant called Evan Jones as witness, and plaintiff caused roars of laughter by shouting out, "No, call Probert first."

His Honour reminded the plaintiff that defendant was conducting his own case.

Evan Jones was engaged to remove Hann's goods into the house that Kramsky was leaving. Witness heard the bargaining as to the glass, and saw one sovereign paid on account.

W. Probert, landlord of 214 Penrhiwber Road, corroborated previous witness's evidence. He could not remember any transaction about gas fittings.

Judgment for plaintiff.

The 1911 Census

1911 was the year of the UK national census, and finds 10 people living at 214 Penrhiwceiber Road, a terraced house with six rooms. The three downstairs rooms could have been a kitchen, a sitting room & a bedroom possibly for Jack, later to be joined by Betty after their marriage in 1911. The three upstairs rooms would have been bedrooms, the main one for Solomon & Bashi and their youngest child, while the other two bedrooms housed the remaining six children.

NAME AND SURNAME	RELATIONSHIP to Head of Family	AGE (last Birthday) and SEX.		PARTICULARS as to MARRIAGE.					PROFESSION or OCCUPATION				BIRTHPLACE	NATIONALITY	LANGUAGE SPOKEN.
		Ages of Males.	Ages of Females.		Completed years	Total Children Born Alive	Children still Living	Children who have Died	Personal Occupation.		Whether Working at Home.				
1 Solomon Kramsky	Head	46		Married	26	8	8	40	Glazier	7 4 0	at home	Russia Resident	Russian Russian Jew	English
2 Beatty Kramsky	Wife		44	" "	26	8	8					"	Russian	
3 Jacob Kramsky	Son	25		Single					Furnisher dealer	Own a/c		" "	Russian	
4 Minnie " "	Daughter		15									" "	Russian	
5 Rachel " "			12						School	390	0	" "	"	
6 Slima " " "			10						School			" "	"	
7 Reatien " "			8						School			" "	"	
8 Beatrix " "			4						School			Glamorgan Penrhiwceiber British		
9 Abraham	Son	6							School			" "	"	English
10 Samuel Kramsky	Son	2										" "	"	

Solomon is the Head of Family and a "glazier" (self-employed). Jacob is a "furnisher dealer" (also self-employed). Apart from the youngest, all the children up to the age of 12 attend school. Minnie, who is 15, is not listed as working; she probably helped her mother at home, and her brother and father at work.

Everyone apart from the youngest 3 children, who were born in Wales, were born in "Russia", with their nationality as "Russian Jew". In the days of the Russian Empire, that could mean almost anything from the Baltic to the Black Sea!

30 and 185 Penrhiwceiber Road these days.

3. From Russia

Bashi & Solomon with their 3 youngest children, and Jack & Betty's eldest child Isy.

A note on the back of this photo - found by Arlene in 2005 – is written by Harry Pelta. It reads : "Rabbi Kramski. Young boy is Istie Kramsky. Bishopston."

Solomon & Bashi

Solomon Kramsky was born on 24th June 1864 in Bratslav, modern-day Ukraine; his parents were Abraham Kramsky and Sarah Doshifsky. Or in 1865 in Warsaw, Poland, depending on which set of documents are to be believed. Solomon was described as a tall gingery man with brown eyes (but measured at 5'2"), and a clever scholar who taught Hebrew in Odessa, and in Wales, and later in New York. Indeed he was known as "Rabbi Kramski" in Swansea, but that may be an exaggeration.

Bashi, the daughter of Moshe Melman, was born on 18th June 1866, (again, documents vary). Bashi was a short fairish woman with blue eyes (short being 4'8").

Solomon & Bashi married in around 1883, again maybe in Warsaw; perhaps they moved south to escape from a nasty series of pogroms that took place there from 1881. In any case, they were in Bratslav in the mid 1880s, a town famous as a seat of Hasidic Judaism.

Jack, their first child, was born in 1886 in the town of Pechera, a dozen miles from Bratslav. They remained in the area for a few years, as Jack was at least partly educated in Bratslav. Some time before 1895, the family moved to Odessa; there is a gap of 9 years between Jack and his siblings Minnie, Rachel, Lena (Selena), Rebecca & Abraham, who were all born in Odessa between 1895 and 1904. Their last two children, Beatrice and Samuel, were born in Wales in 1907 and 1909.

Around 1905 or 1906, Jack had saved enough money to pay for all of his family to emigrate from Odessa to Wales. British Parliament had only recently brought in the "Aliens Act" of August 1905 as a measure against immigration; it has been estimated that between 1881 and 1905, around 150,000 Jews fleeing Tsarist Russia settled in the UK, as well as large groups of Lithuanians, Poles, Germans and Chinese. Before 1905, no formal documents were required for a newly-arrived person to live or work in the UK, but from then on, a passport had to be shown. Moreover, each person was required to possess at least five pounds in cash. It was not unknown for a five pound note to be passed around during immigration checks!

There was another snag though, as Bashi was initially not allowed entry to Britain because of a weak eye. Never one to shy from a fight, Jack enlisted the help of Baron

Melchett to take her cause to the House of Lords. Baron Melchett was in fact born Alfred Mond, of a German-Jewish family; he was later to be owner of the Brunner Mond chemicals company (now owned by Tata); as well as being MP for Swansea, hence the connection. Naturally they won the case, Jack being able to look after his parents and siblings from the money he was earning in his shop.

Solomon used to help Jack by carrying panes of glass around on his back, going door to door asking for repairs. Of course, if a local boy had (accidentally) thrown a rock through a window recently, there would be more windows to repair...

Vita's mother, with Vita's sister and children (most of their names are unknown.)

Dear Ester
I send you as a keep-sake this photo
Us family 36 years ago

from me Fany

Mam's mother & sister & her children

Vita

Meanwhile in Odessa, a girl called Vita Dashefsky was working as a dressmaker. She was very fond of art and music, and used to visit the opera whenever she could afford to. As the situation for Jewish people worsened, she realised she had to get away. One day she was shown a picture of a handsome young man with a waxed moustache, and rather liking the look of him, it was decided that she should go to England to meet him.

Since there weren't a huge number of eligible girls living in the mining villages of Wales, Jack's parents worried that he would marry a non-Jewish girl. Money was sent over for her to buy a ticket, and despite her friends' protestations that she wouldn't be happy in Wales, over she came, telling herself that if she didn't like it, she could travel onwards to her relatives in America.

When she arrived at Paddington station, with nothing but a scrap of paper with "Penrhiwceiber" written on it, there was no one there to meet her, and she spoke not a word of English! Just when she'd given up hope, a young man with a moustache and a boater came running down the platform, waving frantically. They liked each other straight away, but it must have been quite a culture shock to find herself in little Penrhiwceiber, after the cosmopolitan Odessa.

Betty used to make her own beautiful dresses - they used to call her the princess. When she arrived at the cottage, there was the mother-in-law to be, with a dead baby in the bed with her. So naturally they thought "Oh well, we've got a very nice servant here," and right away put her to work - cleaning, cooking, mending, and generally looking after things.

Studio photographs of Jacob & Vita, around the time of their marriage.

On 28th December 1911, Jacob Kramsky (24, Bachelor, Furniture Dealer) & Vita Dashefsky (21, Spinster) were married at 214 Penrhiwceiber Road, "according to the rites and ceremonies of the Jewish religion". Jack's father Solomon is listed as a "Glazier"; Vita's father is listed as "Benjamin Dashefsky, deceased".

No.	When Married.	Name and Surname.	Age.	Condition.	Rank or Profession.	Residence at the time of Marriage.	Father's Name and Surname.	Rank or Profession of Father.
54	December 28th 1911	Jacob Kramsky	24 yrs	Bachelor	Furniture Dealer	214 Penrhiwceiber Rd Penrhiwceiber	Soloman Kramsky	Glazier
		Vita Dashefsky	21 yrs	Spinster	—	214 Penrhiwceiber Rd Penrhiwceiber	Benjamin Dashefsky	deceased

1911. Marriage solemnized at Penrhiwceiber in the Parish of Pontypridd in the County of Glamorgan

Married in the house 214 Penrhiwceiber Rd according to the rites & ceremonies of the Jewish Religion by certificate

This Marriage was solemnized between us. Jacob Kramsky / Vita Dashefsky X — In the Presence of us. Morey Freedman / H. Corb. — W. Jacobs (minister) / M. Fishout (Secretary)

[Esther]

There were in-law problems right from the start. Betty couldn't speak a word of English, and was treated like a slave. But she liked her father-in-law, who was a sweet old boy. She was blamed for everything - they used to call her 'Stumme' ('The Dummy'). She refused to talk until she could speak English properly - she could hear that the locals spoke a rough language, with a lot of swearing, because of the men working in the mines - it wasn't a very nice place.

When Betty became pregnant with her first child, she went on hunger strike. She told them "If you don't take me away from your parents, I don't care if I live or die." Her weight dropped from twelve stone to seven, and they sent for the doctors for a suspected case of consumption (tuberculosis)

When the doctors realised that she didn't like her in-laws, they said "Well, you'll have to take her away. She can't stand living here. They treat her like a skivvy, and she'll die if you don't take her away." It must have been terrible for her, coming from a life of fun in Russia. After that, Jack had to find a little house for them, so at least they weren't living on top of each other; but he had to look after both families.

Probably Penrhiwceiber.

Someone cared for this photo, repairing it at least twice.

214 Penrhiwceiber Road is long gone, but the houses opposite still stand.

4. On the Moldavanka

Конная, уг.Коблевская, 22   Конная, уг.Коблевская, 23   Конная, 24

Starokonny flea market on the Moldavanka, Odessa

Odessa

Solomon & Bashi appear to have moved to Odessa some time before 1895, and stayed there for a few years until emigrating to Wales in around 1906.

Solomon had a brother named Lev, who was in Odessa during the same years. It is unknown whether they had travelled there together from Pechera, or if Lev was already living in Odessa. In any case, Lev was married to Nechama, and they had children including Mordechai (Motiya), Shimon (Sioma) and Rosa (Shoshana).

Solomon & Lev's parents were Avraham – rabbi and school master – and Rachel.

There is some confusion as to whether Avraham & Rachel are actually Solomon's parents (as I have it), or Sioma's parents (as Alexandre has it). Rather than brothers, they could be uncle & nephew – or cousins.

Sioma, the Undefeated

Sioma was born in Odessa in 1905, the son of Avraham & Rachel, and lived through many of the "great events" of the first half of the twentieth century. In the depths of Tsarist oppression of the 1910s, and the Bolshevik Revolution of 1917, he married his childhood sweetheart Tsipora, with whom he emigrated to Palestine in 1924.

They worked the land on the newly-founded moshav of Nahalal, with a mixture of European, Russian, Arab & Jewish friends, and enjoyed life by the sea at Bal Galim near Haifa, where Sioma's mother Rachel had settled – his father had refused to leave Odessa.

Even though Lev never left Odessa before his children, it seems that he moved via Turkey to Moldova, where he died in around 1930.

In 1928 their only son Alexandre was born in Nahariya. When civil war broke out in Spain in 1936, Sioma and some of his friends, including two Palestinian Arabs, joined up with the Dombrowski brigade to fight against Franco's fascists. After Franco's victory, Sioma crossed into Vichy France, but was captured and sent to Gurs internment camp, and later to Le Vernet concentration camp. Desperately trying to escape, he finally made his way to Paris, where he died in 1960.

Sioma's recollections, as told to his son Alexandre Thabor, in 1958, are currently being made into a book due to be published in 2020 in French. The following extracts are translations from his manuscript into English.

Extracts from "Sioma l'insoumis", i.e. "Sioma the Undefeated"

We lived in a large house on the outskirts of Moldavanka, the Jewish quarter of Odessa - Odessa, our mother, open to a warm sea ... The city nourished our dreams, our hopes and our fantasies. In its low-lying, beautifully decorated buildings, separated by a range of small courtyards, a whole world of shopkeepers, craftsmen, rabbis, workers and smugglers worked. All of them, years later, were exterminated in the Nazi Holocaust.

Our apartment was located on the first floor. The entire ground floor was occupied by your grandfather's school, Avraham Kramsky. Two large windows overlooked a courtyard that accommodated the children during recess. Your grandfather had a class of about twenty students whose parents were all friends. He also learned to read and write Russian, Hebrew and Yiddish. It inculcated a secular culture both Russian and Jewish. From my earliest childhood he told me the story of Moses, the liberation of the Jews from the Egyptian yoke, of King David and King Solomon. He spoke to me about Isaiah, Ezekiel and especially about Amos, his favourite prophet, who he called the "first revolutionary worker." Thus he bequeathed to me the supreme qualities of Judaism: this permanent anxiety for freedom, this refusal of all injustice.

During our walks in the alleys of Moldavanka, people greeted him. He stopped to speak to them, worried about their health, that of their children, and deplored their submission, their resignation in the face of suffering. "Ein lanou brera", they replied, "we have no choice." He tried to create a feeling of revolt in them. The police watched him, for his socialist engagements were, in their eyes, eminently suspect. The rabbinate honoured him and accused him of leading a Heder, a religious school, without being himself a rabbi and, above all, not teaching the Talmud or the Torah in the strict sense. Suffice to say that he was considered an atheist and a "red".

As for my mother, Rachel, your dear savta, you knew her well. At the time, she appeared to me great, beautiful and solid. She managed the house, which was not easy. Some days we did not have much on our plates. On Thursday, she went to the main market of Privoz to buy provisions for the Shabbat dinner. She sometimes took me there, and I must admit I loved it. It was like a huge playground for me. I took advantage of the tumult and the shouting, to steal small objects. Then I mingled with the Jews and Christians who chatted, joked and sometimes scattered for a kilo of potatoes or two chicken legs. Savta, for her part, found a privileged contact in the person of a farmer, who regularly brought her a basket of vegetables, eggs, some herbs and a loaf of bread. Sometimes he even offered her a handful of sprats, a turbot, or a bonito. My mother and the man I took for a farmer never stayed long together. Much later I learned that in the basket, under the bunches of vegetables, were hidden revolutionary pamphlets. I had no idea of the struggles that occupied my parents, the reasons they had for saying yes to the Bolsheviks, and not to the Tsar. Carefree, I'd rather have fun, go downstairs to class, abandon myself to the stories my father told us about Bar Kokhbah and Rabi Akiva, the two heroes of the Jewish insurrection against the Romans, Or about Tarass Boulba, that warlike Cossack imagined by Gogol. I then used the break times to play at Cossacks with my comrades. But of all the stories he told, my favourites were those concerning the Baal Shem Tov, the rabbi who founded Hasidism, who was an inexhaustible source of spiritual and entertaining anecdotes.

"Your grandfather Avraham said that our ancestors had bequeathed us a permanent anxiety and a refusal to adapt to the realities of our time. It is this inheritance that we have received: an insatiable quest for freedom. Since the Prophet Moses and Bar Kokhba, the man who took up arms against the Romans, every compromise appears to us like a prison. We refuse to endure oppression and serfdom. We refuse to believe that there are no other choices than engulfing one's life in work. We refuse to suffer from morning to night with only the hope of keeping a job to survive ... It is impossible for us not to fight the injustices."

There was a demonstration ... a procession of strikers ... who were singing, laughing, and raising their fists. I saw Grisha with his satchel. My father was not far away, he had found other teachers in the procession. My mother was on my right and I squeezed her hand so as not to lose her. A shot rang out... blood flowed from his chest. The crowd froze before opening this child on the ground. [..]. A rebellion on the march which was to spread and submerge the whole of Ukraine. My father, with infinite tenderness, said to me: "Sioma, the time has come for the Jews to know anger."

My world had shattered. For several days, I neglected my lessons and I buried myself in excursions to the flea market for Yeshua. My father was worried. Money began to seriously run out. The parents of many pupils were unemployed, hungry, and humiliated. To get through, they preferred to send their children to work rather than to school. This put my father in a rage. Whatever the material problems, a child must learn to be a good Jew at school rather than on the street! As for the hostility of the rabbinate and the tsarist police, Avraham did not worry about it, but his wife was tormented by it. I thought then that Yeshua could be the master of the situation. I was sure that he would get along with my father and that between the two of them they would find a solution. I cannot tell you what part Yeshua played in the fulfilment of my destiny; I know only that it was important.

Yeshua Varchevsky was the smartest dealer in Odessa. He was about forty years old, fairly handsome, his face already wrinkled, but full of life and fire. He lived in a little house which the Cossacks had sacked one day whilst he was shopping in the flea market. They had killed his wife, his two children, and had destroyed all the objects and paintings he had stored there. Yeshua had not become discouraged, devoting himself even more ardently to the flea market, specializing in the research of antique objects, learning their history.

Yeshua knew everybody and everybody came to see him to buy, exchange and especially sell rare items, paintings, clothes, old books, porcelain, clocks... Whenever we brought him a bauble, he would look attentively at it, turning it over and over in his hand, pouting, but would not let anyone leave without a few rubles. The adults took advantage of his generosity by sending him their children, before whom Yeshua, in remembrance of his own, was completely disarmed. Thus, little by little, the children began to work for this antiquarian dealer of Odessa. For a few rubles a week, they neglected their schooling and went all over the city, visiting houses, searching through rubble, and looking for objects that might interest him. Yeshua lent money to those who really needed it, from the little money that these items brought him. As for himself, he lived very poorly, like all the Jews of Moldavanka. But he possessed the talent of finding rare objects which he would sell in the Upper Town, among the bourgeois and the aristocrats. Everyone loved him and welcomed him with pleasure, for he always brought with him his great sense of humour.

My father and Yeshua had a tacit alliance: the children must go back to school, otherwise the dealer would not buy anything from them. They had to arrive there at seven in the morning and finish at two. Then Yeshua invited them to breakfast, after which they were free to go hunting and sell him their afternoon finds. He went so far as to propose to them to work on Shabbat and the eve of Shabbat, triggering a terrible scandal. The rabbinate was up in arms. But the parents did not care, the children had fun browsing the city in search of treasures, and my father was delighted to see his pupils come back.

This agreement between the dealer and the professor produced a strange effect on the children. After their quest for Yeshua, in the evening or sometimes the next morning, my father made them sit around him and looked at them one by one. He took his time, then, in a calm voice, awakened their conscience by revealing to them his own convictions. The children would come up with astonishing questions: "Why does a religion of love and joy inspire intolerance, malice, hatred, violence, killings and massacres of innocent people?" And more personal questions, such as a little boy who asked "What is Jewish? Is it because I am? What does that mean: I am Jewish?"

At the time, I used to ask myself exactly the same questions. Was I Jewish because I was the son of Savta? Because I was Jewish? What is the meaning of this question? What does our desire to endure, not only as human beings, spirit and seed, but as a Jew mean? These existential questions have never been answered satisfactorily for me.

Avraham, delighted with his association with Yeshua, soon offered him the opportunity to integrate the flea market into his pupils' curriculum and become their melamed, the

"Professor of the History of Objects". Through the antiques trade, it would be possible to teach children the Jewish history of the city, of Ukraine and Russia. He had at his disposal a sumptuous collection of illustrated books devoted to the history of Odessa. Yeshua could speak to the children of Armand du Plessis, Duke of Richelieu, the first mayor of the town, of his great labours and exploits; and of the history of the Emperor Alexander II, his reforms and his assassination. Not forgetting Peter the Great and the history of the Cossacks. These magnificent editions had everything to please the students, but also their parents.

Everything went for the best within what looked like a community. We divided as accurately as possible the revenue of our sales between the needs of the school, those of the families and those, of course, of Yeshua. It was a very happy time and I was preparing to take the high school entrance exams. Thanks to the lessons my father had given me, I was a year ahead. However, the prejudices of the downtown goys had not disappeared. Avraham and Yeshua were very quickly identified and denounced as dangerous elements. The righteous goods rivaled themselves of slanders, demanding their arrest, even accusing them of misappropriation of minors. Without knowing it, we were reliving the trial of Socrates. Faced with this cabal led against the school of Avraham, the parents of pupils remained steadfast and did not wish the children to abandon their double occupations. Everyone wanted to keep the community alive. The anti-Semites again asked the police to intervene. A fanatic had even conceived the idea of murdering Avraham and Yeshua, burning down the school and the house. They had even made an attempt which fortunately had failed.

From that time on, my father and Yeshua decided to arm themselves. They were joined by parents of some of the pupils. We were surprised to see our Jewish and non-Jewish high-city guests come to support us and take a stand at the entrance of the school, ready to fight. Anxious, Yeshua advised Avraham to leave Odessa without delay for New York. He knew a lot of people, collectors, lovers of Russian art. He promised Avraham a school in Brooklyn where he would be free to practice his style of teaching. In Odessa he risked his life. He was embarrassing too many people. Even some of the communists had been irritated by his unusual activities. They suspected him of forming counter-revolutionary intelligences. But Avraham believed that there was no danger in Odessa, since he was doing nothing reprehensible, and that he was in favour of Lenin.

More worryingly, he had suffered two heart attacks while teaching in class. He was now in frequent pain. He felt weakened, breathless, often unable to speak for a few minutes before recovering. Savta had begged him to reduce his class to a dozen students. But my father refused to do so, not wanting to see the joie-de-vivre of this community of pupils disappear. He preferred to die rather than forget his past or flee his future. He had learned that one cannot escape one's destiny. One day, two policemen came to seek Yeshua. One of his customers had lodged a complaint, accusing him of theft, deception of merchandise and misappropriation of minors. It was the first time I saw a man arrested for saying yes to the dreams of the children, not their suffering and hunger, not their slavery because they were little Jews from Odessa. It was on the basis of this blatant injustice that, suddenly, a flash of lightning gave me the idea that I, too, had the right to say no, to arm and to defend myself, to kill if necessary.

I was too upset, too enraged to be able to justify this thought; I only wanted to avenge myself for the tortures and humiliations. It was during this period that I first thought of joining the Communist youth organization of the Party, the Komsomols, to learn how to handle arms. But I was still too young.

For our third meeting, my father invited me to his home in Argenteuil. He wanted to show me his diary, the boxes of photographs where he had stored his memories. He wanted to tell me about his adolescence and his youth. Sioma lived in a modest villa lined with rosebushes, located rue Baratier, a stone's throw from the Seine.

In May 1958, France was going through a serious crisis, including the Algiers putsch, the Maurice Audin and Henri Alleg cases, torture, the return of de Gaulle, strikes and demonstrations. My father opened the door with a big smile, hugging me as always with warmth, in the Russian way. Lea was on duty at the hospital and little Andre was in bed. He had prepared a very simple meal: beautiful chicken legs, fried potatoes, a salad, a plate of cheese, a bottle of Evian and a bottle of Saint-Émilion. After dinner, we went to his office, a glass of wine in his hand. He chose a pipe from among a dozen, suspended from a rack placed below a reproduction of the dove of peace of Picasso. Once at his ease, in his sofa, he resumed his story.

Our wounds did not scare my parents at all. Abraham, on the contrary, made us understand that for the Jews the war against the Black Hundred** was not over, that we must arm ourselves yet more. And my mother helped us wash, put compresses on our wounds, saying: "The intolerable is to wait without fighting that they massacre us, the Jews of Odessa ...". Turning to Abraham, she said: "As Ezekiel says, he only performed a sacred act for a sacred purpose."

** ultra-nationalist, Pro-Romanov/Tsarist, anti-semitic pogroms, etc

We wanted to change the air, live and love quietly. Olga and Yuri, friends of Odessa, had written us from Palestine to invite us to settle in Nahalal where they had created their own farm. They had several hectares, cows, a henhouse, and horses. They were happy and they made us want to know this bliss.

Thus, all three of us, Gideon, Tsipora, and I, have decided, almost without explicitly saying so, to make Aliyah. We knew the situation in Palestine. The conflicts between the Arabs and the Jews for a country which belonged to both peoples. Two peoples, condemned to live together, could only agree on one thing: to drive the English out of this land. In February 1924, we finally scheduled our departure for Haifa aboard Jerusalem.

The day before we left, we all gathered for supper: Rachel, Moura, Josef, Gideon, Yeshua, Tsipora, his father and the inseparable Rabbi Ben Yakov. The table was sumptuous. Savta had taken out the most beautiful cutlery and the food was much better than usual. The conversation revolved around Eretz Israel and the situation in Odessa.

Avraham gave us his latest recommendations. He warned us against Jewish chauvinism, against those who use fear, hatred and force to satisfy their interests, which cause the two peoples to be killed, Jewish and Arab. According to him, the attitude of the Yishuv, the Jewish community established in Palestine, towards its Arab neighbours was not only political, but was an integral part of Judaism. Just as anti-Semitism undermined the credibility of Christian principles, thereby becoming a Christian problem, so the Jewish attitude towards the Arabs was a questioning of Judaism and thus became a Jewish problem.

"The essential thing, my children, is not how the Bolsheviks govern us, or how the English govern Palestine. The essential thing is not the regime of oppression we are under, or that of Stalin or Trotsky will take power now that Lenin is dead. The real problem is that of our dejection and resignation. It is against this docility that you must fight, against accepted servitude. We are everywhere in civil war, between Russians and Ukrainians, between Jews and Arabs ... We need a policy, Sioma, a policy that gives rise to the desire to live together, the desire for a common society. In Eretz Israel this should be possible. Here, we must especially beware of the moustached man... of Stalin..."

5. Towards Swansea

Betty with Isy in his pushchair, 1913

In 1912, Jack and Betty left Penrhiwceiber, and for the next couple of years lived in Newport and Llanelly, until they found themselves in Swansea, where at least some of the family lived until the 1950s.

"Jack Ramsey" can be found working as a "Drapers Traveller" in Newport in September 1912, where their first child Israel (Isy) was born.

It didn't take long for Jack to appear in the newspapers – this time in the Cambria Leader. In July 1915 he made a small donation of 2 shillings to a committee which had been formed in Swansea, *"for the relief of the unfortunate Jews in Russia and Poland, who are dying in thousands from hunger and poverty, after being robbed and driven from their homes. [..] sufferings greater than at the time of the Inquisition."*

SOUTH WALES WEEKLY POST, SATURDAY, OCTOBER 9, 1915.

LLANELLY RUSSIANS.

PROSECUTIONS UNDER ALIENS' ACT.

At Llanelly on Wednesday, the following were proceeded against for offences under the Aliens' Registration Act:—Mary Toplis, Old Castle-road; Solomar Kramsky, 33, Prince of Wales-road, Swansea; Arthur Nurse and Jose Daniel Marin, 54, Nathan-street; Elizabeth Jane Davies, 4, Stanley-street; August Silg, 4, Stanley-street, and Jack Kramsky, 13, Cwm-road, Swansea.

Detective Hodge Lewis said that two Russian subjects lodged with Mrs. Toplis, but there was no register. He saw Soloman and Jack Kramsky later in the day, and they produced papers showing that they were Russian subjects. The forms had not been filled in.

Mrs. Toplis was fined £1, and Soloman and Jack Kramsky ordered to pay 5s. 6d. each towards the costs.

Arthur Nurse was fined £1, and Marin 10s. Davies and Silg each had to pay 5s. towards the costs.

In 1915 both Solomon & Jack were fined for not registering as aliens.

At the outbreak of the first world war in 1914, all non-British citizens over 16 were required to register at local police stations and to demonstrate a good character and knowledge of English.

THE CAMBRIA DAILY LEADER, TUESDAY, JULY 8, 1919.

And in 1919 Jack was sued for missing and broken jam jars!

IN THE DISTRICTS.

SWANSEA.

At Swansea County Court on Tuesday Messrs. Morgan Bros. sued Jacob Kransky for £5 12s. 4d. in respect of jam jars delivered in a quantity too few, and in a damaged condition. His Honour gave judgment for £2 11s.

Kramsky or Ramsey?

Jack & Betty's two eldest children, Isy & Sarah, who were born in 1912 and 1914, were born Ramsey; at that time, Jack & Betty were Ramsey too. However, after his prosecution in 1915, they were legally required to use the Kramsky name, and stuck with it. Of their seven surviving children, Isy reverted to Ramsey; Sarah emigrated as Kramsky; Morry changed from Kramsky to Ramsey; and Esther, Annie, Frances and Leah stayed or married as Kramsky.

Between 1912 and 1919, Kramskys senior & junior are found in various places such as Hewertson Street in Newport in 1912-13 (road now demolished), in Llanelly in 1915, and in various places in Swansea - Cwm Road, Neath Road, and Rock Street.

Not enough lead

In 1918, while doing business as a general dealer or "marine stores", at his home at 1362 Neath Road, in the Hafod area north of Swansea town, Jack was in trouble with the law again. According to the 1903 Act, it was illegal to deal in small quantities of metals - iron (under 10 cwt), lead, zinc, etc (under 1 cwt) or copper (under 56 lb) - without being licensed. A cwt is an imperial "hundredweight", meaning 112 lb (8 stone). A "qtr" is a quarter, meaning 28 lb (2 stone).

In the Petty Sessions of 22nd July 1918 at Swansea, Jacob Kramsky is up against 4 charges. The spoken testimony of PC Wm Francis, which was speed-written verbatim in long-hand, can be found in the court record book.

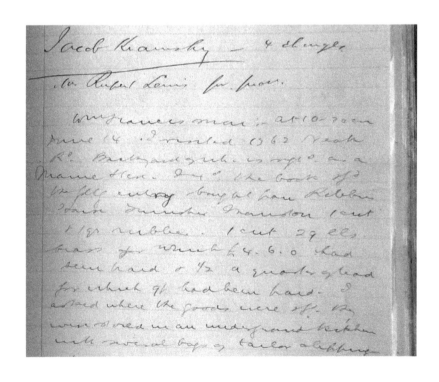

… at 10.30am June 14. Kramsky: I reside 1362 Neath Rd. Backyard of which is regd' as a Marine Store. [..] bought from Robbins of Morriston 1 cwt 1qr rubber, 1 cwt 29 lbs brass for which £4.6.0 had been paid & 1/2 a quarter of lead for which 9/- had been paid. I asked where the goods were if they were stored in an underground kitchen with several bags of tailor clippings a place which had not been reg'd as a place of deposit.

At 7.10 20 June evening with PC Harris I visited the premises & saw Kramsky. He was at that time attending to several customers. He said what can I do for you. I cautioned him told him who we were. [..] in the book an entry he had purchased 1 cwt 1/2 qu rubber 1 cwt 29 lbs brass & 1/2 a qtr of lead. He replied I made a mistake in writing down weight of the lead I should have put down 1/2 cwt that is what I bought. Here is the receipt for it, which he produced. I asked him if he had a permit [..] He replied I have not got one. I told him he would be reported for buying less than 112lbs of lead. He replied Well I shall plead ignorance I thought I was allowed to buy 1/2cwt. I am sorry if I have done wrong. Also told him he wld be reported for failing to register underground kitchen as a place of deposit. He replied That is all I can say is I am quite ignorant to all. I have no one to advise me.

On July 1. I saw Kramsky at Goldblum stores. He had just delv' a quantity of stuff there 1 cwt 3 qtrs 10lbs scrap brass. 2 qtrs 10lbs of zinc & 105 lb of lead. I said where have you bought this lot from. He replied I bought it of Robbins Morriston. We then visited his stores [..] I pointed out to him that on the 13 June he had purchased from Robbins 56 lbs of lead. 1 cwt & 29 lb brass & today you have sold 105 lbs of lead to Goldblum & 1 cwt 3 qrs 10lb scrap brass. I cautioned him—He hemalaled for some time & said all I can say is it is what I had from Robbins. I told him I was not satisfied & should report the matter. For his failing to enter purchases of 49lbs of lead & 2 qrs 9 lbs brass bet'n 14 June & 1 July 1918.

He made no reply.

Verdict—Guilty on all 4 charges - 1. Failing to enter purchase of 1/2 cwt of lead. 2. Failing to enter particulars of same. 3. Purchasing lead of less than 112 lbs. 4. Failing to register as a Marine Dealer or Metal Dealer.

Each conviction carried a 40 shilling fine, or 21 days imprisonment. It is not recorded which he chose.

6. Prince of Wales Road

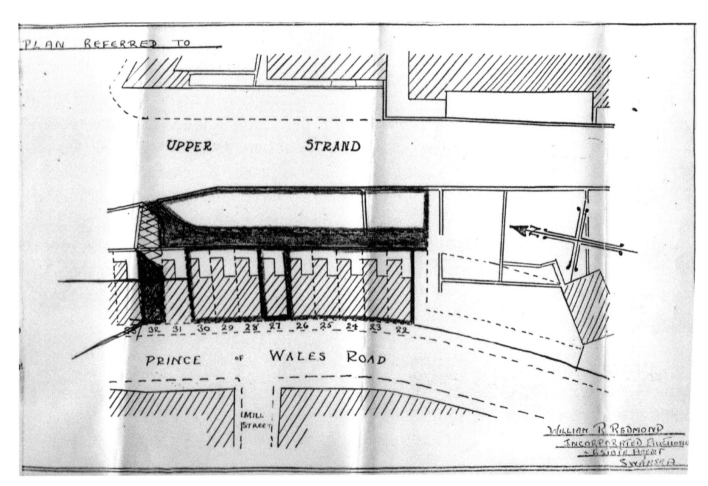

32 Prince of Wales Road, with Upper Strand below.

Prince of Wales Road

Prince of Wales Road was once a busy thoroughfare, running diagonally off the High Street, just north of the railway station, up to the Hafod Bridge. The road was built up in the 1880s by the "Swansea Improvements and Tramway Company", who laid down tramways all over Swansea and the surrounding areas, naming it grandly after the future Edward VII. The Swansea to Morriston tramway ran up and down Prince of Wales Road until the rails were pulled up in 1937.

As strange as it sounds, the road was originally paved with wooden cobblestones, which were cheaper than granite, avoided the noisy clatter of iron-rimmed wheels and horseshoes, and even protected against vibration from the tram tracks. One side-effect, however, was the wood's absorption of "horsey fluids", giving off noxious smells, especially in the summer months.

Once home to more than a dozen shops and small businesses, the end of the trams in 1937 signalled the decline of this once bustling street. The road suffered damage in the blitz of 1941, and the collapse of several houses in 1950. When the New Cut Road was built in 1991, the Hafod Bridge half of the road was wiped off the map. It now lies buried beneath the bushes, and traffic islands, of the new road, leaving just a no-through road beyond Swansea High Street Station.

In February 1920, Jacob Kramsky moved into 32 Prince of Wales Road with Betty and their four young children. To finance the purchase, he took out a private mortgage for £300 with Major General (later Colonel) Strick of Edinburgh. He also took out fire insurance to the value of £600, in the name of "JAMES KRAMSKI", with an annual premium of 14 shillings and 10 pence which included "other perils" such as explosions, riots, articles dropped from aircraft, and earthquakes.

In 1931 Jacob Kramsky, Rag & Metal Merchant, took a new mortgage for £400 with "The People's Land Building and Dwellings Company Limited", a grand name for a small company which went out of business soon afterward. In 1934, after Jack's second bankruptcy, the house was transferred into Betty's ownership, where it remained until 1965.

The Palace Theatre

At the High Street end of the road is the Palace Theatre, built in 1888. In the early 1900s performers such as Charlie Chaplin & Lily Langtry appeared on its stage, as did Anthony Hopkins in 1960. Later it became a cinema, a bingo hall, and a nightclub, before falling silent in 1991; it is now in serious danger of collapse.

In 2019 Swansea Council announced a £5 million pound redevelopment of this Grade II listed building, an "iconic Swansea landmark."

The "Palace Theatre" on the corner of Prince of Wales Road & High Street. Above in 1904, and below in 1915.

Sadly decaying in 2016...

But hopes of revival in 2019?

The Shul

Prince of Wales Road is situated in the Greenhill area of Swansea, home to so many Irish immigrants in the second half od the 19th Century, that it was known as "Little Ireland". In the late 19th and early 20th Century, an influx of Jewish immigrants began to change the makeup of the area.

A minyan had existed in Prince of Wales Road since 1896, made up mostly of the poorer immigrant Jews from eastern Europe; Ashkenazi, Orthodox, and Yiddish-speaking. This group was distinct from the Goat Street synagogue, where the more established Jews prayed. As the Jewish community grew, the Minyan was renamed the Swansea Beth ha'Midrash, and a purpose-built synagogue was consecrated there in 1907, built with donated bricks & stones.

In 1913, many of the inhabitants of Prince of Wales Road were Jewish; shopkeepers and tradesmen. In the 1930s & 1940s, many of them could afford to move to the better parts of town. The BhM continued to exist until 1955, when it merged with the Swansea Hebrew Congregation. The building was unoccupied for a few years before it was finally sold in 1961.

Prince of Wales Road Synagogue when it opened in 1907; and the building in 2014.

[Esther]
Though my father was Orthodox, he couldn't afford to take Saturday off - a very busy day - there were nine of us to keep. we always kept a very kosher house, and we kept all the festivals - my father became a leader of the synagogue - the Beth Midrash where it was in walking distance of all the people who lived there. My father sang like Caruso—you could hear his voice like a bell above all the others.

The JC

Published continuously since 1841, the Jewish Chronicle has been the newspaper of record for Jewish life in the UK, marking many occasions both happy and sad, and news both local and from afar. Of course, Jack Kramsky would not be restricted just to the secular press, appearing more than a dozen times in its pages.

June 1916. "Fund for the Relief of the Jewish Victims of the War in Russia" - many individual members of the Swansea Committee made donations, including: J.Kramski (13 shillings) and S.Kramski (2 shillings, 6 pence).

This fund was set up to help Jewish families emigrate from Russia, away from the violence, famines, and anti-Semitism which had rumbled on since the revolution of 1905, and the war from 1914.

April 1921. "The Jewish War Memorial" - many individual donations, including "J. Kramsky, Esq, £5, 5 shillings."

This "memorial" was a fund set up for Jewish teaching and training, in memory of the Jewish soldiers who had died in the First World War. It took a further 40 years to actually build the memorial, when it was raised in Willesden, North London in 1961.

SWANSEA.

Under the auspices of the Beth Hamedrash and the Zionist Society, a meeting was held for the purpose of presenting a Golden Book Certificate to Mr. M. Cohen for his services to the Beth Hamedrash, of which he has been *Gabbai* for seven years. Dr. Annie Foner presided, and the presentation was made by Mr. J. Kramsky, the present *Gabbai*.

Rabbi Nathan Milichowsky, of Palestine, addressed a meeting of the Zionist Society last week. At the close of the meeting 35 dunams of land were subscribed for, and the town is being canvassed for further donations. The Rabbi also addressed the members of the Beth Hamedrash. Rabbi Milichowsky addressed a gathering at Llanelly, where 25 dunams of land were promised. Further donations are expected. A Commission was formed to carry on the work of the Jewish National Fund.

January 1924. Two things to mention here—

Firstly, a Gabbai is a "Shamash" or "a person who assists in the running of synagogue services" - a "Jack of all trades" perhaps?

Secondly, this Rabbi Nathan Mileikowsky was a famous and fervent promoter of Zionism. He was born in Russia, and became director of the Mordechai Krinsky Hebrew Gymnasium in Warsaw, before moving in 1920 to Rosh Pina in Galilee. In the 1920s and 1930s, he preached his message from Siberia to San Diego, and at least once in Swansea! Incidentally, he signed his writings as 'Netanyahu' ("God-given"), the surname still used by his sons & grandsons, one of whom is Benjamin, twice prime minister of Israel.

September 1924. "London Federation of Ukrainian Jews" - A nationwide campaign for funds, J Kramsky being on the committee of the Swansea campaign.

May 1939. "The Council for German Jewry" - "Messrs J Kramsky, Ltd (Swansea) - £2, 2 shillings"

After the racial Nuremberg Laws of 1935, and with much difficulty, the CFGJ ultimately helped almost 100,000 Jews leave Germany before WW2.

February 1940. "£250,000 Appeal for the Purchase of Land in Palestine for the Settlement of Refugees.

"Swansea—Messrs J Kramsky, Ltd - £169, 12 shillings, 4 pence" - one of the largest donations.

February 1944. "Jewish Relief Team goes abroad". A team of seven from London & elsewhere to work in the Mediterranean, including "Mr Israel Kramsky, of South Wales". "Emphasis is laid on the fact that the team is not going to do specifically Jewish relief work, but will help all in need."

June 1947. "Jewish Relief Workers" from Stepney, attached to Brady Clubs, including "Izrael Kramsky from Wales"

June 1954. As the Beth Hamedrash's existence comes to an end, it was intended to send the assets to Israel in order to establish a synagogue. However it took over seven years to conclude the arrangements.

BETH HAMEDRASH FOR ISRAEL

" Transferred " from Swansea

From our Correspondent

SWANSEA

The contents of Swansea Beth Hamedrash are to be transferred to the Convalescent Home of Mifal Hatorah at Givat-Ora, near Jerusalem. This signals the final closing of the Beth Hamedrash, which, founded in 1906, supplementary to the Swansea Hebrew Congregation's synagogue, developed as a separate congregation, catering especially for immigrants from the Continent.

The premises have not been used at all for more than a year. There has been a drift of the community westwards, leaving Prince of Wales Road, in which the Beth Hamedrash is situated, with only two Jewish families. At one time there were more than 30.

Relics of Chevra Shass

Mr. Lewis Goldstone, President of the Beth Hamedrash, stated this week that Mr. J. Kramsky, acting as Secretary, had written to the Chief Rabbi of Israel seeking advice on the transfer of the whole of the assets, including the Ark, Almemar, seats, Sifrei Torah, and valuable books—the last named being relics of the Chevra Shass and its library, established at the Beth Hamedrash some 40 years ago. Also to be transferred will be the proceeds of the sale of the Beth Hamedrash freehold premises.

In connection with the transfer arrangements Mr. Barry Mindel, Secretary of the Mizrachi Organisation, visited Swansea last week.

The agreement reached between Mr. Mindel and the Trustees refers to the shipping of the contents to Israel "for the purpose of establishing a synagogue in the name of Swansea Beth Hamedrash, perpetuating its name and that of its officers and members."

February 1955. Building to let.

PRINCE OF WALES ROAD, Swansea. Freehold building. approximately 1,500 ft; suitable for warehouse or club premises; vacant possession; £2,500, freehold.—N. Rosen, 277, Whitechapel Road, E.1. (BIShopsgate 8017.)

Swansea

SIFREI TORAH TO STAY

From our Correspondent

Three Sifrei Torah, together with silver appurtenances, originally at the Swansea Beth Hamedrash—which has been closed for some years—have now been handed over to Swansea Hebrew Congregation.

All three had been held by old members of the small congregation, and when the Beth Hamedrash in Prince of Wales Road was finally closed after being without a stipendiary official for a long time, tentative arrangements were made with the Mizrachi Organisation to send the Sifrei Torah to Israel. They will instead remain in Swansea to be used on behalf of the surviving members and the children of the founders of the Beth Hamedrash.

May 1958. Since 1954, the Torah scrolls had been looked after by "old members"; they are now given to the Swansea Hebrew Congregation.

Jack Kramsky had died on 11th April 1958—perhaps these two events are related?

December 1960.

Request for the scrolls to be returned.

Following a meeting of surviving members of the long defunct Swansea Beth Hamedrash last week an approach has been made to Swansea Hebrew Congregation for the return of a Sefer Torah which, it is stated, was promised to Mizrachi for shipment to Israel.

May 1961. The assets are now to be sent to a Yeshiva in Netiv Meir, near Mount Herzl, in Jerusalem. Mizrachi is the worldwide religious Zionist organisation, founded in 1902, with a UK branch opening in 1936. They provide ideology and guidance for Modern Orthodox Judaism. Bnei Akiva is their youth movement.

SWANSEA

Synagogue assets for Israel

From our Correspondent

Almost exactly seven years after a formal agreement was reached between the then members of Swansea Beth Hamedrash and the Mizrachi Federation, the fifty-year-old Beth Hamedrash is to be formally transferred to the Bnei Akivah Yeshiva, near Mount Herzl, in Israel.

The Swansea Beth Hamedrash was founded by immigrants from Tsarist Russia and other parts of Europe, who moved to Swansea and built themselves a place of worship and a Talmud Torah.

Most of the original members and their families have now gone, many of them to the western end of the town. Many members joined the local Hebrew Congregation, whose synagogue was more conveniently situated. Mr. Lewis Goldstone, President of the Beth Hamedrash, with one or two supporters tried to maintain services on Shabbat and Festivals, but the loss of older members made this impossible.

A meeting decided to sell the building and transfer the proceeds to Israel. Mr. Barry Mindel, General Secretary of the Mizrachi Federation, attended a special meeting on May 31, 1954, at which formal agreement was reached. Now, after seven years, the legal formalities have been overcome. The building has been sold and new trustees have been appointed.

7. Esther's Childhood

Prince of Wales Road

When I was a child, my mother lived in a bungalow with all the children. My father had a metal store and rough people used to come in and weigh metal. My father had had a bulldog at one time, and that had died. They also had a chick and that had grown up to be a beautiful cockerel, and as it was always scratching we called it 'Maria from the Barnyard'. One day my mother said "It's no good - every time anyone passes the bungalow to go through the shortcut, this cockerel flies out at them." "I'll tell you what I'll do," my father said. "I'll take it down to the stores." These were open stores, with no fences or gates round them. Well, that cockerel became better than any watchdog - if ANYbody came near my father and it thought they might attack him it'd fly at them - it was really fierce.

In the house where I lived, there were ten of us - us seven children, Mum and Dad, and a maid. We lived in this small house in Prince of Wales Road - which sounds much posher than it actually was - and these houses were quite small. I don't know how we all managed, with three bedrooms and one bathroom. My mother and father slept in one, with always a baby; then the rest of us made do with the other bedrooms. Anyhow, we all slept. We were the only ones to have a bathroom - my father had one made out of half of one bedroom - you can imagine the size of the bedroom - Isy slept in that room. Then Sarah and Frances slept together. I slept with Morry - I slept at the top of the bed and he slept at the bottom. We used to fight like hell over the blankets - I'd pull it up, and he'd pull it down - this went on all night until one morning I found him missing. He'd gone into Isy's room, and from then they decided they would make a bedroom downstairs in the middle room, which nobody really used - we only used it for doing homework. So we put two beds in that room, for Isy and Morry to sleep together.

Then we always had a girl working for us - Florrie. Florrie came to us when she was about thirteen - her stepmother brought her. They always used to take these girls from orphanages or disturbed families, and they would place them in Jewish homes - they knew that we would look after them well. So she became like our adopted sister, and through her, we had a very happy childhood—instead of fighting with each other, Florrie would try to make us laugh. I have a feeling that our mother loved her more than all the children, really. If ever - when she got older - she left us after an argument with our mother, and went to work for somebody else, my mother used to break her heart—we had to go and find her to bring her back again.

We had a telephone number, which was connected with my father's business, which was more or less round the corner - he was a metal merchant's. Our phone number was '2754'. I can remember that, but I can't remember my children's numbers. If the children misbehaved themselves, my mother would say "I'm going to phone your father!" It would frighten us to death, but he never even smacked us - one look from my father kept us quiet. It was the wrong way to bring up children, really, because we could never really get close to him because of that.

We had a kitchen that we all ate in, which was quite a big-sized kitchen. Then there was the scullery, which had a boiler in the back - not like the modern boilers, but a big, brick-built boiler, and the actual boiler - made of zinc I suppose - was inside. Then the fire was lit underneath it to heat the water, and my mother would do a week's washing in that boiler. In that scullery was a mangle, and no matter what the weather was like, I'd mangle every Monday morning. The back yard had the toilet in it - I don't suppose it had real toilet paper - you were lucky if you had newspaper in those days!

Although it was a small backyard, there was a chicken shed there, so we kept our own chickens. if Morry was naughty - he was terrified of these chickens - he was such a good boy, really, my mother would threaten to put him in the chicken-kutch - kutch is the Welsh word for shed. I remember her saying "If you're not good, I'll put you in the chickens' kutch!" He was terrified of it - it was dark, and all these fluttery old things lived in ther!

Our houses in Prince of Wales Road were built right on top of another row of houses called the Strand - at one time there must have been a river there. My father had a big scrap-metal business down in the Strand, and he also owned some arches. These arches, which had the scrap stored in them - were right underneath our house. In one of these arches was a room, an attic, where my brother Isy opened a boxing ring. At the time the fascists were coming in, so Harry Pelta and Isy opened this gymnastic room, and they used to train there. People didn't know that Jewish boys could be tough like that - Harry Pelta was the weightlifting champion of Wales. Isy and Morry were both in his weight-lifting team as well, but Harry was the real champion.

Anyway, before they had converted that particular room, when I was a girl, we had another girl working for us - after Florrie had left us - whose name was Dolly. We had a big kitchen range with a fire-guard in front of it to stop the coals going into the kitchen, and Isy used to sit on top of this fire-guard. One day he was messing about and he fell over the rail right into the space between the fire and the rails. My mother left him there, for a while, to teach him a lesson. He had his feet up on the guard, and he was lucky that the fire was pretty low, otherwise he would have burnt his behind.

This Dolly Currant only lived round the corner from us, but she used to come round and stay with us and mind the children. She used to go home to sleep every night - she wasn't like Florrie; Florrie was like our adopted sister. Anyway, she had to boil up all the water - she had this bucket of water and she put it on the open fire and I was playing in front of the fire-guard - I can still remember that; I must have been about four years old - and the bucket of boiling water fell over and scalded my leg. I must have screamed the place down, because my father, who happened to be in the arches, saw the hot water going down through the ceiling, and he came running home - he must have heard my screams - and I remember, I can still see it if I close my eyes—that they wheeled me in a pram up to the chemists. They didn't bother with doctors in those days—the chemist was like our doctor in a way. The chemist was right near the Blacks - the Blacks family had ten children and we had seven, so everybody used to mix us up, as there were only a few Jewish families living in that area; they always used to say "Are you one of the Blacks girls or the Kramsky girls?"

c1925 - Needham the Chemist - known as "The Doctor".
Here in his doorway at 39 Neath Road; a 5-minute walk from Prince of Wales Road.
Ninety years later, the shop is still a pharmacy.

Anyway, I was explaining as we passed the Blacks' shop and they saw me in this old-fashioned push-chair with my leg up in the air. I've still got marks on my leg - I'd forgotten how I got those. So of course, I went to Needham the chemist - I remember him putting stuff on it, and bandaging it up - and the Blacks girls came out; I must have been screaming all the way up the road - they were like our family, so they all came up to the chemists with me. I remember that shop, and I remember he had some sweeties in a box there, and he gave me some sweeties. I had my leg up for quite a long time until it healed up - I was lucky really. Anyway, we didn't see Dolly any more after that episode - I think she got the sack!

In our road, there were lots of shops as well as houses - I remember there was a sweet shop. At one time my father was very religious, and this woman used to come in to our house to turn the lights on and off, and light the fire - I think we used to call her 'Mrs. Moker with the Poker'. She would come and sit all day long, and poke the fire - she was a 'Sabbath Goy' - that's all she would do all day! She was a sweet old lady, come to think of it, with the most wonderful complexion, and she owned the sweet shop down the road. Sometimes she'd let me come and help her - I loved helping there, because she'd always give me a couple of sweets - it was always nice and clean in there.

The Neighbours

- Flood—they sold bread pudding at a penny a piece;

- Pearlman—Jack gave their sons Charlie & Honky £5 to buy film for their first Brownie camera.; they became the Pearl of Pearl & Dean;

- Jacobs—kept chickens that the shochet used to kill in the back yard;

- Belkin—next door neighbours, sold pickled herrings in the front passage; old Mr Belkin taught the BarMitzvah portions;

- Samuels—daughter married a man who looked like King Kong in Goat Street synagogue;

- Mrs Hughes—made Esther & Sarah their first dresses for a dance;

- Kalpus—Mrs Kalpus got a sewing needle stuck in her arm, and they couldn't find it; Morry's nose broken by Mona Kalpus while she was playing netball;

- Belkin—Shmuel, brother of the other Belkin, came into our house, put a cigarette in his pocket and fell sleep on the settee; was killed later when the houses collapsed;

Captain Jack

Then somebody said: "Jack! I've got a wonderful idea! I've got two fishing-smacks - if you go partners with me, we'll go out into Swansea Bay, and Bristol Channel, and we'll catch a lot of fish. We'll come back to the docks, and we'll sell that fish, and we can be very rich, very quick!" Luckily we always kept the scrap business going, or we'd have been broke by now! So once again he went partners, invested a lot of money again to buy these boats. So he hired sea-captains to go fishing, and sometimes he went out with them, just for the thrill of it. Then came the big day, when they came back with a really good catch of fish.

He got quite excited about this - he had people at the docks ready, and who else was at the docks but the inspector of taxes - my father had broken a law—again! He didn't know you had to have a licence to go out fishing in fishing-smacks! So he had to take all the fish and take them back and empty them back into the sea! He was heartbroken. So this went on - another case to fight - he didn't think you had to have a licence to fish! It was free - God's own creatures in the sea. Anyway, that wasn't the law, so once again, ignorance of the law didn't mean exemption - you're still guilty, you should have found out first.

So those two big fishing-smacks were sitting in the docks, and then his partner - a very clever man - said "I don't really want those smacks, will you buy me out?" he said. "My wife is ill, and if you get new engines, you'll be able to use them for pleasure boats - take them for trips across the Channel." Anyway, it didn't work out, he bought him out, and I remember coming home from London, and seeing - it was just before the war - those fishing-smacks, and all I could see was timber, all pieces of timber, driftwood - those were the fishing-smacks. A storm had come up that year and broken them to bits - and crashed them against the dock walls. And that was the end of the fishing smacks!

8. Lime Kiln Yard

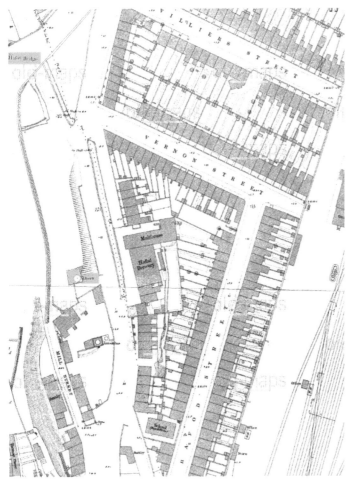

The Lime Kilns in Upper Strand - still in use around 1890

Strand, Swansea, around 1937

The Old Flint Mill

Beneath Kramsky's scrap yard, if anyone cared to dig, would be found many layers of history.

The first layer would be the eponymous "Lime Kiln", where limestone had been burnt in order to produce quicklime, a key ingredient in cement, hugely important for the construction industry.

The Swansea-to-Morriston tramway ran across the Hafod Bridge from the 1890s onwards. In years gone by the Bwrlais stream ran beneath the bridge, feeding the Aberdyberthi Mill; the bridge was then known as the Aberdyberthi Bridge. The stream has long ago been diverted, and the bridge is above the confluence of Upper Strand & Cwm Road. As long ago as the 16th century, the Mill had milled corn, but latterly it was known as the Flint Mill, grinding flints to be used in the manufacture of the famous Cambrian Pottery.

Article in the Cambria Daily Leader, 8th April, 1893

The old Flint Mill, the pile of old ruins which, lying snugly at the base of Aberdyberthi Bridge, attracts the attention of SO many of the passengers of the Tramway Company, is to be razed to the ground. Councillor J. M. Mayne, to whose enterprise the erection of the good-looking, but peculiarly built row of houses fronting the bridge is due, has purchased from the Duke of Beaufort the land on which the old mill stands, and within a month it will come down, and with it will go the last of the buildings connected with the manufacture of Swansea china, and some of the most interesting old landmarks of ancient Abertawe that are now extant.

For four centuries the old pile is said to have been in existence, being the greater part of the time in use as a corn mill, until the manufacture of ware sprang up here, and then it was used for grinding the flint with which was made the 'warranted iron ware,[..][Considering its age, the walls are in an excellent state of preservation now, and round about are many mementos of the period of its useful existence ; a great water-wheel, for instance, twenty feet in diameter, with a shafting — a solid casting — two feet thick. There are parts, too, of the old engine, which was constructed when steam power was introduced into the premises [..] and a good many of the huge flint boulders with which the flint pebbles used to be ground, some of them half worn away by the friction, and with a surface as smooth as a lithographer's stone.

Above the water-wheel there is a culvert, through which there used to come the water from the old mill pond, now dried up and made the site of a lime-kiln ; and below there is another culvert to carry away the water to the canal — a culvert through which a man may wheel a barrow. The miller's house, and one of the great pan rooms in which the milling operations were carried on, are now occupied as a smithy.

Limekiln Yard

Jack Kramsky ran a scrapyard at the old Limekiln Yard from around 1920 until at least 1950. It was situated in Upper Strand, directly below their house in Prince of Wales Road, and adjoined the arches under the Hafod Bridge. He also rented "Number 8 Arches" which was behind the yard, and directly beneath the row of houses above.

In 1920-1922, he is a "rag and metal merchant" in Upper Strand. However in 1923-1926, he is *"Employed as manager of a Marine & Metal Stores, at Upper Strand, Swansea, by B.L.Lewis, Arcade, Llanelly"*. By 1929 though, he is *"J Kramsky, general merchant"* in Upper Strand.

Over the years, he bought & sold an amazing variety of new and second (or third)-- hand materials, from rags, jam jars, metals and timber, to bicycles, cars and billiard tables. Not to mention rabbit skins.

"Marine Stores" originally meant any ships' supplies, such as rope, anchors, food, etc., but evolved into referring to second-hand ropes, cables, sails and so on. Eventually the term came to mean "sellers of any old junk."

Extract from "Bleak House" by Charles Dickens, published 1852-1853

> She had stopped at a shop over which was written **KROOK, RAG AND BOTTLE WAREHOUSE**. Also, in long thin letters, **KROOK, DEALER IN MARINE STORES**. In one part of the window was a picture of a red paper mill at which a cart was unloading a quantity of sacks of old rags. In another was the inscription BONES BOUGHT. In another, **KITCHEN-STUFF BOUGHT**. In another, **OLD IRON BOUGHT**. In another, **WASTE-PAPER BOUGHT**. In another, **LADIES' AND GENTLEMEN'S WARDROBES BOUGHT**. Everything seemed to be bought and nothing to be sold there. In all parts of the window were quantities of dirty bottles--blacking bottles, medicine bottles, ginger-beer and soda-water bottles, pickle bottles, wine bottles, ink bottles;

In Dickens' book, amongst Krook's collection of papers is the key to the case of Jarndyce vs Jarndyce. Or perhaps Kramsky vs Rabbit Skins...

J Kramsky Ltd

The Wall Street Crash of October 1929 sent shockwaves around the world, and triggered 10 years of uncertainty, leading up to the Second World War. The Great Depression of the 1930s hit industrial areas of Britain the hardest, with high unemployment and low inflation.

In June 1930, Jack decided that a Limited Company would limit the risk to his personal assets. Should anything happen to the business, the liability would be restricted to the company's assets, and the shares worth £250. Perhaps he had seen the writing on the wall, as in May 1933, Jacob Kramsky, "Marine Store Dealer and Colliery Proprietor" was made bankrupt by court order.

THE LONDON GAZETTE, 19 MAY, 1933

No. 1,781. KRAMSKY, Jacob, 32, Prince of Wales Road, Swansea, and carrying on business at Upper Strand, Swansea. MARINE STORE DEALER and COLLIERY PROPRIETOR.

Court—SWANSEA.

Date of Filing Petition—April 25, 1933.

No. of Matter—7 of 1933.

Date of Receiving Order—May 17, 1933.

No. of Receiving Order—8.

Whether Debtor's or Creditor's Petition—Creditor's.

Act of Bankruptcy proved in Creditor's Petition—Section 1-1 (G.), Bankruptcy Act, 1914.

Extract from "Mervyn's Lot" (2002)

by Mervyn Matthews (1932-2017)

At the other end of the social scale was Mr. Kramsky, thought to be Russian, and the main 'rag and bone' merchant in the Hafod. In fact he specialised in scrap metal and every boy in the Hafod knew his great yard down the Strand. Anything that was the least bit rickety would be derided as having come from there.

"Where did you get your bony-shaker then, been down Kramsky's 'ave you?"

Jack Kramsky, dour and red-faced, clad invariably in a dark blue suit, would sit day after day in a booth at the entrance to his domain, apparently oblivious to the stench of dirt and rusting metal which it exuded. He would argue endlessly over the loads of scrap that the rag-and-bone men brought in on their carts. His business, I imagine, throve greatly from the war munitions drive, and behind the scenes he may have been quite well off.

One day I slipped into his yard, partly out of curiosity, partly in the hope of finding some old tools. He took no notice of me whatever because he was dealing with a couple of young men who had just dumped their scrap on his weigh-bridge scale, which was set in the earthen floor. Their horse clinked its hooves restlessly outside as Kramsky slid the weight deftly along the gradations on the bar. "A hundredweight," he declared, and reached for his wallet.

"No, it's not," said one of the men, "I saw the bar. It was well over."

Mr K's English wasn't very good, but he swore with great fluency. "Oh f—king hell," he said. "Jesus Christ. No it wasn't. The bloody weights and measures inspector was here, see. He couldn't get over it. The wind blows under them sodding scales and makes the weight look more than it is. Honest to Gawd! But I'll keep my word, I'll give you what I said" (which was, of course, less than they wanted)."

Swearing.

While Jack was certainly known for his colourful language, it seems very doubtful that he would have used the exact blasphemous profanities that Mervyn remembers. When he swore, it was almost always in Yiddish – for example "stuckfleish mit oigen", "geh shlegs der kopf in der wand", "oi'll rip you in sieben stickele"* - never in English. This seems to be more a case of a 10-year old Welsh boy guessing what the mysterious words might have meant in English.

* literally "piece of meat with eyes", "go and bang your head on a wall", "I'll rip you into seven pieces"

Extract from "Down the Memory Lanes of my Hafod" (2008)

by J Ramsey Kilpatrick (1929-2007)

School days 1934-1943

The boys in the street used to make trolleys or bone shakers, what we called 'old Boneys', from planks of wood and two sets of pram wheels with axles. We'd go hurtling down the street, dragging our boots all the way until we came to halt at the bottom.

For me, though, the bit I enjoyed most was actually making the cart; collecting all the bits and pieces and using the tools hanging up in the shed to drill and cut and hammer until the old Boney was more or less roadworthy. Old prams were in shorty supply because they'd be passed from one household to another but if you were lucky you might pick up a matching pair of pram wheels for a few coppers from Kramsky's, the scrap merchant down on the Strand.

One time I managed to save up my pocket money and I bought a bicycle frame and some wheels for 6/6d from Kramsky's. Uncle Reg decided it was probably time I learned how to build a bike and he took me off to buy the other bits and pieces.

Extract from "My Greenhill Far Away" (2002)

by Brian Ahearne (b.1925)

Brian's ancestors migrated in the 1840s from Ireland to the Greenhill part of Swansea, which was predominantly Irish for most of the 19th Century.

At the top of the Strand was a scrapyard. It was a very famous scrapyard. Famous, that is, to the Rag and Bone fraternity. The name of this establishment was 'Kramski's'.

Mr Kramski, the proprietor, was a Jewish gentleman, as his name would imply. He was the very epitome of a Jew, with long black overcoat, and a bowler hat. He was an astute businessman, as indeed he would have to be, dealing as he did with the many rag and bone men who were his customers.

His yard was the depository for the gleanings of this mobile army of scavengers. Most of these ragged-arsed subreptionists were illiterate, but let me tell you, they were all conversant with the current prices of the London Metal Market, and could manipulate a very keen price from old Kramski.

I was glad when I was old enough to go to Kramski's yard, for the constituent parts of a 'Boney'. This popular mode of transport consisted of an old bicycle frame, bereft of its wheels, pedals, seat and brakes.

By substituting the original wheels for a pair of old pram wheels, and a saddle made from an old potato sack, which was folded up and tied to the frame with string, you were the proud owner of a 'Boney', and you were mobile.

This ungainly contraption was propelled by gravity, when travelling downhill, and by 'scooting' it along when on the flat. We would travel miles on these unroadworthy bone-shakers, oblivious to the dangers of non-existent brakes, etc.

Another mode of transport, much enjoyed by the boys, was the "Trolley" or gambo. This was the Car version of the Boney. The manufacture of this vehicle called for more expertise than knocking up a Boney. It required two pairs of pram wheels, complete with their axles. A short plank of wood, about three feet long, formed the chassis.

Trolley Race - Aberdyberthi Street

Extracts from "The Hafod 1920s-1950s"

Mrs Meg Thomas (nee Morse), writing in 1993 :

I was born in Cwm Terrace, in the twenties, and if ever there was a district rich in characters it was the Hafod.

I was one of 13 children. We all attended Hafod School. At one time I could boast that I had a sister in every class.

We lived near Jack Kramsky who had a 'scrap yard'. I remember that my mother used to let us have the skins after she had removed them from the rabbits. Jack Kramsky used to give us a penny for the skin. He was quite a kind man, he turned one of his stables into a place where the unemployed youths could go at night to box or play cards, a kind of gymnasium. It was somewhere to go off the streets.

Landore Cinema (Neath Road. Opened 1913. Closed in 1938)

The cost of admission, which included a bar of chocolate or nougat was 2d in old money. Youngsters would wait anxiously to see if their Mother could afford the 2d.

The fear of disappointment would generate tremendous activity on Saturday mornings, and "Kramsky" would have a queue of children offering rags and scrap metal, some with bated breath as they waited for him to make his judgement as to the worth.

I wonder if he knew that an afternoon of pleasure depended on his generosity. Rabbit skins were a different proposition as they had a fixed price of 1d. Some would collect returns, pop bottles to return to the shop from which they were bought, others would collect empty beer bottles to

Landore Cinema, also known as the "Bug", is about a fifteen-minute walk up Neath Road from the yard in Upper Strand. The cinema opened in November 1913, and closed just before the war "for the duration". It never reopened, although the building still stands and is a listed building.

In a 1914 directory, there were 19 cinemas in Swansea alone. Did the kids in those other 18 queues sell their scraps to "Kramsky" too?

Extract from "Pineapple Sundays" (2008)

by Haydn Williams (b. 1936)

(1946)

I was ten and a half now, growing up and exploring the wider world away from the Hafod, the park and the Great Tip. [..] On the very first day of the holidays we decided to set off on a hunt for jam jars in a bid to make some money. Jack Kramsky the scrap metal and rag and bone merchants were paying a penny for a pound jar and a halfpenny for a half-pound jar.

(1950)

[..] cobbled surface of the Strand which led down to the lower part of the town. It was mainly a commercial district with no houses as far as I knew. Opposite Kramsky's rag and bone yard there was a sharp bend to the left, leading back to the Hafod. Past the Hafod Bridge I continued down the Strand. This had once been a flourishing riverside area, but there was now a sense of decay about the place with many run down and derelict buildings. The only thriving businesses were those of the rag bone and scrap metal merchants occupying the arches underneath Prince of Wales Road. Further along there was a narrow side road leading up to a bridge where I crossed over the main railway line before emerging by the Palace Theatre on the fringe of the town centre.

Without any warning in the early hours of September 9th 1950, three houses in Prince of Wales Road collapsed, sadly resulting in the deaths of seven people. The houses, which were built over huge arches slid, in an avalanche of rubble, into The Strand below. These arches were occupied by the businesses of a number of rag and bone and scrap metal merchants, places where I and many children like me in the Hafod had often taken empty jars, bottles and the occasional bag of rags to be exchanged for a few pennies. [..] People in the town remained in a state of shock for a long time afterwards, often comparing the tragedy to episodes during the wartime blitz.

Lifting Weights

Harry Pelta

Harry was one of the Jewish boys who ran the gym with Isy & Morry, under the arches in Upper Strand. He became the heavyweight weightlifting champion of Wales in 1935, while also learning the tailoring trade. He later went into the jewellery business, running a shop in Swansea.

After the scrap business was moved further down the Strand in 1943, it is not known if they kept hold of the old yard. If so, perhaps they passed it on to a friend who shared a love for weightlifting, for example...

Terry Perdue

Born in Swansea in 1941, Terence Robert John Perdue (Terry), appears to have run a scrap dealers' on the Lime Kiln Yard from the 1960s until about 1980. Another colourful character, he was part of the British Olympic Weightlifting Team in both 1968 and 1972, coming 10th in the heavyweight class both times. He also has an entry in the "Great Jews in Sports" encyclopaedia (published 2000).

In the words of Dave Prowse (champion weightlifter and the real Darth Vader) :

Terry was an enormous bull of a man, a scrap dealer, and he didn't have a clue about the technique of the lifts. He was like an unleashed tiger on the platform and was difficult to coach and control. It was all brute force and ignorance in those early days, and nine times out of ten his technique was so bad and his behaviour so erratic that he failed to register a total. [..] his appearances on the platform were always a bit of a joke and brought great hilarity to what was normally quite a serious occasion. Sometimes he lifted enormous weights and at other times he'd fall flat on his arse with them. We never knew what he was going to do, but it certainly made for interesting competitions.

"Vault", reporting on the World Weightlifting Championships in Havana, Cuba :

Oddly, the popular hero of the final night was one of the colorful—if not always effective—Britons, Terry Perdue. He is bearded, stuffs 320 pounds into a six-foot frame and could be played in a film by Peter Ustinov. Like his teammates, he was expected to contribute little more than laughs to the proceedings. [..]

A scrap dealer in Swansea, Perdue had been arrested in 1971 along with two other men and charged with the theft of 41,000 pounds of metal. He was sentenced to four years in prison, but he kept up his training there and after serving nine months was acquitted on appeal just in time to join the Olympic team and appear in the games. The joke with the British lifters in Havana was, **"Hurry up and lift. Perdue is coming. We might not have any barbells left." [..]**

Instead of entering upon the stage in deliberate fashion and walking back and forth cautiously during the three-minute time period allotted for a lift, he strode briskly from the wings like a fretful Ustinov, then paced back and forth in quick march. Where other lifters would stop and carefully rub their hands in one of the two bowls of chalk on either side of the stage as if engaged in some mysterious rite, Perdue would have none of this. Without breaking stride he would suddenly flick a giant paw into a bowl, raising clouds of white dust. The Cubans, who love the impulsive gesture, would roar their appreciation. [..] Perdue next would eschew the customary approach to the lift. He would suddenly cease his marching, wheel and practically run to the bar, seize it and hurl it over his head. Thunderous applause. He earned gales of laughter when he slipped once and tumbled on his back, and he almost brought down the house when he cleaned the bar to his chest only to have it appear to become ensnarled in his beard.

Purdue can be seen in "Visions of Eight", a documentary film made during the 1972 Munich Olympics, as one of the athletes in the "Strongest" segment.

Terry died in 1998, and is still remembered as a character by local businessmen.

Terry Perdue Jr

Terry Jr followed his father into weightlifting, into the scrap metal business, and also into the tax evasion business. He represented Wales in the 105kg+ class at the Commonwealth Games in 1994, 2002 and 2004, and was a reserve at the Olympic Games in Greece in 2004. As of 2016, he is currently in prison for VAT evasion, after failing to declare over £3 million in payments.

Natasha Perdue

After becoming national Karate champion, Terry's daughter Natasha switched to weightlifting, representing Wales at the Commonwealth Games in 2006, 2010 and 2014, and Britain at the 2012 Olympics in London.

Later years

Terry Perdue (Sr) is listed as bankrupt in 1981, after running the Yard as "Perdue & Morris" and under various other names. After that Raymond Lorey took a turn, as "Millbrook Metals" and/or "Morriston Metals", also filing for bankruptcy in 1988. Lastly in the early 1990s, "City Metals" seems to be the final business trading there before the area was redeveloped.

**This patch of land was once home to Limekiln Yard.
Now home to teenage girls smashing bottles.**

New Cut Road

Swansea is a constantly evolving city, and in about 1991 the New Cut Road was extended, requiring the destruction of about 40 houses in Prince of Wales Road—some of which had been knocked down as unsafe in the 1950s & 1960s. Much of the rubble was pushed down the hill, and as a consequence the remaining businesses in that part of Upper Strand were closed down.

Hafod Bridge, seen from Upper Strand.

On the Hafod Bridge

This fairly nondescript view tells many stories!

- We are standing on the Hafod Bridge (old grey bricks). A prominent local landmark since it was built in 1822, it carried the old Swansea-to-Neath turnpike road, and is now a Grade II listed structure.
- We could drive left here, into the New Cut Road, under the railway and towards the retail parks near the river Tawe. After about 20 metres, we would be driving almost exactly over (or under) the spot where 32 Prince of Wales Road once stood, and then under a modern footbridge which is now the only connection between Prince of Wales Road and Upper Strand.
- Beneath the Hafod Bridge is Upper Strand itself, which leads to viaducts on the north side of Swansea (High Street) railway station. The trees on the right cover about half of the site of Lime Kiln Yard—the rest is now buried beneath New Cut Road.
- The road leading uphill between the rows of houses is Vernon Street. When Siegfried Bachenheimer was looking for a more English name, he decided on "Fred Blake". Esther thought he needed a middle name, and suggested "Vernon". A coincidence?

9. Walter's Road

68 Walter Road (on the left) is now a veterinary surgery

Walter's Road

Originally known as Walter's Road, and now known interchangeably as Walter, Walters, or Walter's Road, this is part of the "high road" leading from the north side of Swansea towards Uplands and Sketty, as opposed to the "low road" which hugs the coast to Brynmill, and onwards to The Mumbles.

Soon after being built in the 1870s, the road attracted its first professional critics –

The British Architect: A Journal of Architecture (March 1875)

Perhaps one of the finest thoroughfares in the town is Walter's Road. Here is to be seen a well laid-out avenue, nearly 100ft wide, nicely planted and paved. Of the very many respectable dwellings that, standing within their lawns, skirt this fine street from end to end, there is scarcely a solitary one to be seen whose facade is not of the dowdiest or most vulgar character. A well-designed house here and there would have imparted to the monotonous thoroughfare a wholesome variety; but from end to end of Walter's Road the speculating builder seems to have reigned supreme. One only public structure (the Congregational Church and Schools) lends a partial relief to the dreary blocks of tasteless "villas."

Walters Road c1905. St James Church is on the left, Number 68 is opposite.

68 Walter Road

Situated directly opposite St James Church, number 68 is one of a row of 3 or 4 storey semi-detached villas, which have been occupied over the years by many businessmen and professional types.

Frank Thomas (ophthalmologist) lived here from around 1900-1910. Thomas Meredith Evans lived here from about 1920 until his death in December 1937; he had been managing director of the Beaufort Tin-plate Works, Morriston; at that time the house was known as "Gwernen" (Welsh for 'alder trees').

Despite the bankruptcy a few years earlier, in 1938, the Kramsky family could afford to move to this more up-market house. From 1940-1943, their house phone number was Swansea 4850.

They kept the house until 1946, by which time all their children had left home, and they had moved to the new houses in Bishopston. During the war, it was largely occupied by Jack & Isy, who needed to be closer to their businesses. The rest of the family lived in their bungalow in the less danger-prone Bishopston, especially after the "Swansea Blitz" of February 1941, which had made over 7000 people homeless.

After 1946, the veterinary surgeon Ernest Pugh moved his practice from Mansell Street to the basement of this house, which he later expanded to fill the whole building. In 1956 they became known as "Pugh & Jones", and when Pugh retired in 1966, it was managed by David Jones. The practice is now known as the "St. James Veterinary Group".

70 Walter Road

In the late 1940s, Freddie Blake had offices next door at number 70. It is now home to a firm of architects.

F. V. BLAKE (WALES) LTD
GENERAL MERCHANTS
70 WALTER ROAD
SWANSEA

Thomas the Neighbour

The childhood home of Dylan Thomas at 5 Cwmdonkin Drive is a 5 minute walk away, being just the other side of St James Church. Thomas knew the road well as a boy, and fictionalised the road as "Stanley Road" - in his short story "The Fight", his blackeyed self meets bloodynosed Dan Jenkyn.

Dylan's schoolfriend Mervyn Levy lived at number 56 Walter Road, and his recollections echo Jack's arrival in Wales—

[..] Grandma Rubinstein, who had arrived in Wales from Russia sometime in the 1890's, having booked a passage from Riga to New York. As with many Jews, when her ship docked at Swansea, she was told that she was in America and put ashore.

Dylan also took elocution lessons at number 23 Bryn-y-Mor crescent, just behind Walter Road.

10. The Coal Mine

A disused mining wheel being pulled down

Fields of Coal

In 1853, the South Wales Mineral Railway was opened, to bring coal from the mines at Gylncorrwg, Cymmer and Tonmawr to the docks at Briton Ferry. As the coal became uneconomical to dig, parts of the railway were closed, and the remaining rails were finally pulled up in 1925.

Just east of Neath, between Tonna and Tonmawr, is a coal deposit known as the Wenallt Seam. This was abandoned in 1911.

However... in about 1930, Jack and Isy Kramsky decided to invest in just this coal mine, in the form of the **Wenallt Colliery Ltd.**

It didn't go well.

The Colliery Guardian - March 1933 issue

Opening the defence on behalf of the company and Jacob Kramsky, Mr. Croom Johnson, K.C., said that at no time was there a scintilla of a case against ... defendants the Wenallt Colliery, Ltd., whose mine is situated near Neath, the registered office being at Lime Kiln Yard, Upper Strand, Swansea. The other defendants were Mr. Israel Kramsky, and Mr. Jacob Kramsky, of Prince of Wales-road, Swansea.

In May 1933, as previously mentioned, Jack was made bankrupt. The same went for Isy, who was made bankrupt in July 1935. The paperwork dragged on until at least 1937. This would mean that Isy was about 18 when he became owner of a coal mine, and 23 when he was bankrupted because of it!

THE LONDON GAZETTE, 12 JULY, 1935

KRAMSKY, Israel, 32, Prince of Wales Road, in the county borough of Swansea, MINE OWNER, and lately carrying on business at Lime Kiln Yard, Upper Strand, Swansea aforesaid, and at the Wenallt Colliery, Ton-Mawr, Neath, in the county of Glamorgan.
Court—SWANSEA.
No. of Matter—8 of 1934.
Date of Order—June 13, 1935.
Nature of Order made—That the Bankrupt's application for discharge be adjourned for two years.

Wenallt

The name "Wenallt" translates from the Welsh as "white hill".

In 1933, as this coal-mining business was taking place on the other side of Swansea, a young Dylan Thomas was working on his first book of poetry, and would often spend weekends with his friends Bert & Nell Trick.

Bert recalled "He read it to Nell and me in our bungalow at Caswell around the old Dover stove, with the paraffin lamps lit at night ... the story was then called Llareggub ... that was the germ of the idea which ... developed into Under Milkwood. "

The Welsh title of Under Milkwood is "Dan y Wenallt."

[Esther]

The Coal Mine

My father was always buying unusual things. One day, this man who used to go round selling oil, asked my father: "Would you like to buy a share in a coal-mine?" My father, who was always game, said yes, I don't mind. But what this man didn't know was that this coal-mine was about sixty miles away from where he lived - up in the mountains. It wasn't one where you go down into the pit, like everyone imagines a coal-mine to be. This was a level through a mountain - a level of coal, a coal seam. So my father used to go up every day - it was like a new toy to him - and he used to come home very late. My mother used to sit up night after night worrying about him coming home, sometimes in the middle of winter. There were no lights on the way - out in the country there, miles from anywhere. And then came the big day - we had the coal-miners there. There was the gas-chappie, who goes in with a canary to test if there is any oxygen - if the canary flops and dies, they wouldn't let the miners in to dig for coal.

Anyway, I was working in London then, and came home on holidays, and I said "I must come up with you, Dad, to see this fantastic coal-seam through a mountain." I'd never heard of that - I'd always imagined that you had to go down into coal-mines, and that there was this big wheel to cut the coal - like you see in the movies. I dressed up in my brother's old coat, and a flat cap covering my hair, and my father had the Davy-lamp, and I said "Give me the Davy-lamp, Dad, and I'll go first." The miners had discovered what you call a 'new fall'. What they mean by that is after a very low tunnel, you came to a cavern of coal, which is a tremendous thing. Anyway, I crawled on my tummy - I was quite slim then! - like a snake -you have no fear, you know, when you're young. When I think of it now - this was solid coal - right above my head - you couldn't raise your head up - you had to just crawl for quite a few hundred yards. I remember my father shouting at the back of me "Come back! Come back Esther!" and he's busy coming with me. I suppose he got frightened when he saw me going first. You could just about see me in the glow of this Davy-lamp and then I came to this big cavern - like a hall - it was all cold around me - I couldn't believe that after this long tunnel came this huge cavern - it was like Aladdin's cave of solid coal. There was a trickle of water running down the side - I can still remember it - I could stand up then - I wasn't thinking that I'd have to crawl back again to civilization.

Anyway, this coal-mine nearly made my father bankrupt because he invested a lot of money in it, and I thought 'Oh great! We're going to be able to get all this coal out, we'll become very rich selling coal' But my father didn't read the laws - they said that you were only allowed to take out a ton of coal a week. It was only a small mine, but the men who owned the huge mines, didn't want these tiny mine owners around - they wanted to squash them out. So when we knew we could only take out a ton a week - we could have burnt in our house a ton of coal, with all the fires we had, and the business!

My father really made a fuss over this - he went to court, and he said that it wasn't fair, that they tried to squash him out, that he'd had friends who'd all invested money in the mine thinking that they were all going to be rich. But that was the law, and he went up to the House of Lords to fight it - not for the first time - he was always going up there for something or other, and he said "Just because I'm a Jew, they're trying to squash me out of the coal-mining business!" Anyway, he couldn't win - he lost a lot of money, and so did his friends, who'd invested money in it. So that was the end of his coal-mining career.

11. Saying goodbye

The SS Berengaria in around 1921.

Emigration

On 6th December 1913, Solomon's two eldest daughters Minnie & Rachel boarded the St Paul, a ship of the American Line, emigrating from Southampton on third-class tickets.

Arriving at Ellis Island in the Port Of New York on 14th December, Minnie, 20, was listed as a shop assistant, and Rachel, 18, a dressmaker.

On 6th August 1921, Solomon, Bashi, and their remaining children followed the two girls to New York, arriving there on 17th August, leaving Jack and his young family as the only branch of the Kramsky family still in the UK.

They travelled on the Berengaria, the world's largest ship when it was built in Hamburg in 1912; after the First World War, she was bought and overhauled by Cunard in the UK, and relaunched in 1920, becoming the pride of their fleet.

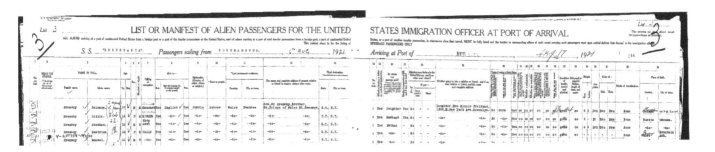

Bessie and Selina, of 34 Prince of Wales Road, embarked at Southampton with 2nd class tickets; Solomon, Lizzie, Abraham, Beatrice & Sam joined the ship at Liverpool, with 3rd class tickets. Third and Fourth class were generally all that emigrants could afford, so the ladies travelling Second class were doing quite well!

Ellis Island

Ellis Island, in the Port of New York, was the entry point for over 12 million immigrants to the USA between 1892 and 1954. People from all over the world would pass through the Great Hall, to be examined for common ailments. It was said that the inspectors could identify almost any condition at a glance, and at a peak of over 2000 immigrants per day, speedy diagnosis was key. After passing through the medical and document inspections, after only a few hours they were released to start their new lives in the United States.

In 1913, the sisters Minnie & Rachel gave their last address as "Mother, Mrs R Kramsky, 13 Brynant Terrace, Swansea", and that their tickets were paid for by their aunt, "Mrs R Greenbeck, Brooklyn, NY". Both were born in Odessa.

In 1921, Solomon, Bessie & the 5 children arrived to join Minnie, now married to Sam Friedman in Brooklyn. Solomon and Bessie stated that they ware born in Warsaw, Poland/Russia. All their tickets were paid for by their son, Mr Kransky* of 34 Prince of Wales Road, Swansea.

Solomon & family

In April 1922, less than a year after arriving in New York, Solomon and family applied for naturalisation as citizens of the USA. Solomon is a Hebrew Teacher, residing in Sterling Place, Brooklyn; he was born on 24th June 1864 in Braslow, Russia (not Warsaw, as other documents say). Bessie and the seven children are all listed, as is Jack who "resides in England". Witnesses are William Bernstecker (PO Clerk) and Samuel Friedman (Ice merchant), husbands of Rachel and Minnie respectively, who are both living at 1206 E NY Ave.

OATH OF ALLEGIANCE

I hereby declare, on oath, that I absolutely and entirely renounce and abjure all allegiance and fidelity to any foreign prince, potentate,

THE STATE OF RUSSIA

state, or sovereignty, and particularly to .... the .... of ....,

of whom I have heretofore been a subject; that I will support and defend the Constitution and laws of the United States of America against all

enemies, foreign and domestic; and that I will bear true faith and allegiance to the same.

x *Solomon Kramsky*

Subscribed and sworn to before me, in open Court, this 20 *day of* December *, A. D. 19* 27

..........................., Clerk.

Success! Five years later, on 20th December 1927, all are admitted as citizens of the United States.

The New York Census of 1925 shows the family living at 1987 Bergen Street, Kings, Brooklyn. Solomon & Bessie (both 58 now) are "Hebrew Teacher" and "House Work"; Rita (21) "Finisher, underwear"; Abraham (20) "Mechanic"; Betty (17) "Operator"; and Samuel (16) - "High School Student."

In the 1930 Census, the family live in a tenement building at 1675 Sterling Place, Kings. Solomon (64) is a "Teacher at a Hebrew School", and Bessie (62) "none"; Rita (25) "operator" and Samuel (22) "paper", live with them.

At the time there were literally hundreds of Synagogues and Jewish schools in that part of New York. Perhaps the Hebrew School was the Chevra Ein Jacob at 1867 Sterling Place, just two blocks away? Or at the Ein Yaakov Orthodox Synagogue at 1811 Sterling Place. There was also a Beth Solomon at 1869 Sterling Place, and a Chevre Sheveth at 1758 Sterling Place too.

On 15th March 1935, Solomon died at home at 1675 Sterling Place; the cause of death was given as "chronic myocarditis, and arterio-sclerosis, with secondary bronchio-pneumonia". Here his birthdate is 20th February 1865, the son of Abraham Kramsky and Sarah Doshifsky, both Russian.

Bessie followed her husband on 3rd February 1939. At the time she was living at 1633 St Johns Place, another tenement one street away from Sterling Place. The cause of death is given as "Coronary thrombosis, contributory factor: hypertension (3 years)." With no date of birth entered, her age is estimated as 60. Her parents are listed as "Morris & Minnie Melnick, both Russian."

Solomon and Bessie are buried together in Montefiore Cemetery, Queens, New York - a cemetery which contains over 150,000 Jewish graves.

The Queen Mary

One year after his father's death, Jack travelled alone to New York for the traditional stone setting ceremony, and to see the family that he hadn't seen for 15 years.

On 27th May 1936, Jack sailed on the maiden voyage of the Queen Mary, from Southampton. The greatest ocean liner of the Cunard White Star fleet, the ship took just five days to arrive in New York; later that year she would capture the Blue Ribands for the fastest Atlantic crossings.

Jacob Kramsky, 53, Metal Merchant, of 32 Prince of Wales Road, Swansea, travelled on a third-class ticket.

The RMS Queen Mary is now permanently moored as a hotel and museum in Long Beach, California.

Betty didn't go to the USA with Jack in 1936, but here she is dressed in "American Style" at around the same time.

[Esther]

When my grandfather had died in America - my father was very upset - and so he went over there - he left his business to his manager - on the maiden voyage of the Queen Mary - an experience of a lifetime - he was wined and dined like a Lord - he had never been abroad before. he was receptioned like a saviour—everybody came to the dock to meet him, as he'd sent them all over.

His mother was ill at the time, and she had a little bundle in her hand - of jewellery which she had gathered up all her life. She called my father to her bedside "This is for you, Yakov." He brought these back to England with him - there was one ring which was to go to me - my sister Sarah was already married and gone to Australia - and I got this big clumsy ring with a black stone and what I thought was glass round it - I never wore it - so Rita borrowed it, and she had it made a bit smaller, but Sheila always said it should have been hers because she was named after my grandmother in Hebrew.

12. Becoming British

Telephone—No.

Telegrams—
"Kramsky, Upper Strand, Swansea."

SPECIALITIES :

Woollen Goods,
Tailors' Cuttings,
&c., &c.

All Orders and Contracts accepted on the understanding that I do not hold myself responsible for any loss or delay arising from contingencies beyond my control, such as War, Strikes, Fire, etc.

J. Kramsky,

RAG AND METAL MERCHANT,

Limekiln Yard & Aich No. 8,

UPPER STRAND,

Swansea,

Feb 13 1922

16 FEB 22

In April 1921, Jacob Kramsky applied to become a British citizen, while living at 32 Prince of Wales Road, Swansea. However, after over two years of letter writing, the application was refused. He reapplied in 1923, and there are many more documents, declarations, and affidavits attached to the second application.

> 2. Causing annoyance by blowing a noisy instrument
>   Llanelly P.S. 9.5.18. Fined 7/6.
> 3. Failing to enter the purchase of ½cwt of lead
>   Swansea P.S. 22.7.1918. Fined 40/- or 21 days.
> 4. Also failing to enter the particulars of same
>   Swansea P.S. 22.7.18. Fined 40/- or 21 days.
> 5. Purchasing Lead of less weight than 112 lbs.
>   Swansea P.S. 22.7.18. Fined 40/- or 21 days.
> 6. Failing to register as Marine Dealer or Metal
>   Dealer, Swansea P.S.22. 7.18. Fined 40/-
>   or 21 days consecutive.

Swansea Police CID produced a special report, detailing all his past transgressions. Presumably in 1918 he was blowing a noisy instrument to celebrate the birth of Anna, just a few days previously! Strangely, he is now "employed as Manager of a Marine and Metal Stores, at Upper Strand Swansea, by B.L.Lewis, Arcade, Llanelly."

Their children's names are Israel Leber, Sarah Leah, Esther, Shendale Anna, Morris, and Fanny. A list of addresses from 1915 to 1921 is given, and affidavits from four neighbours or friends who can vouch for him.

Jack's British citizenship was finally approved in April 1924. And by the British Nationality Act of 1914, as a foreign woman married to a British man, so did Betty.

A passport to nowhere...

There is a curious side note to Jack's application for British citizenship. In April 1922 he obtained a Soviet Russian passport, in his name and six of their children. It is only valid for three months, and only for "abroad" (GB is crossed out).

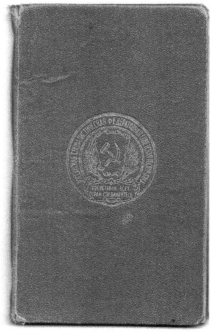
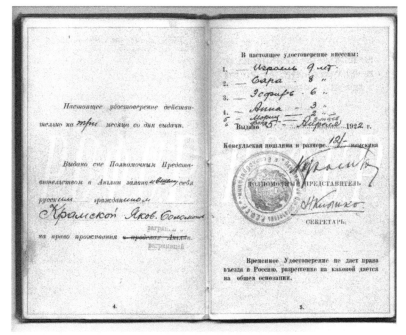

One page of the passport is stamped "American Consulate, Swansea, Wales" and next to it is written "application pending".

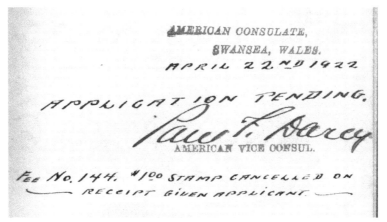

Since he didn't yet have a British passport, perhaps he needed a Russian passport to obtain a visa to America? Or as part of the British citizenship process?

The Kramskys stay in Wales

[Esther]

We were to follow afterwards - we had our passport photos taken - we would have gone; I always remember our father took us all to Swansea Station - that was the first time I ever saw my father crying when we said goodbye - in those days it was like goodbye forever.

Before that I still remember the farewell party - I must have been about six - we went to the house - I remember all these big straw Ali Baba travelling boxes - to get into the kitchen we had to climb over them all - and we had jelly and custard - that was quite an event then. My father decided that we would buy 2 platform tickets, and the rest of us would go on to the next station - Llandore, and we got out there, my father still crying - he had always appeared to me so tough and manly.

Then he found a little scrap yard and decided he could make a living there, and that it was a big risk to go to America, and he would build up business here, and when he could afford it—he would go across nicely, not in a cargo ship like them - in those days it only cost about £5 to get there—so that's why we were Welsh Jews.

13. Holidays in Bishopston

Bishopston Valley in the 1930s

Bishopston

Bishopston lies six miles west along Gower Peninsula from Swansea, whose copper and steel industries put out huge quantities of "dense poisonous smoke". Swansea was known as "Copperopolis" in the 19th century, smelting as much as two thirds of the world's copper, in its 124 metalworks. The industry declined in the 20th century; the Morfa-Hafod copper works being the last to close, in 1980.

While Caswell Bay is public and always busy on sunny days, Pwll Du & Brandy Cove are much quieter since they can only be reached by foot. Pwll Du literally means "black pool", in common with Dublin (Dubh Linh), and Lindow in Cheshire.

From the 1930s onwards, the Kramsky family would often spend their summers in a cottage in Ridley Way, Bishopston, where the air was cleaner than that of Swansea.

Some would say the sun shone brighter too. The children spent many happy summers in their 'paradise', playing on the beaches of Caswell Bay, Pwll Du and Brandy Cove, meeting familiar friends there with their caravans and trailers.

Esther's Stories

The Car

I must have been about twelve or younger, and my father had one of his early cars, and when we lived in the bungalow there was an open field. There were just a few families in bungalows then in summertime. Every time we had a new baby, my father added a new room; it was like The House That Jack Built - his name was Jack.

Anyway there was a lot of area down at the bottom and my father was driving this car round it—so proud he was of this car - he was blowing his horn and everything. All of a sudden the people who were looking out of their windows saw that the tyre's big inner tube was swelling up. He thought they were waving to them, but they were trying to attract his attention to stop the car - the thing could have gone up like a rocket! So my father said "Esther quick - go and get a nail!" He meant a nail to get the air out of the valve. So I came running down thinking, Ooh lovely, and I had my arm up in the air ready to puncture this thing.

The kids were in the car and my father put his arm out the window and started shouting "Meshuggene!" and other words of endearment like that. "Stuckfleish mit Oigen! What are you doing?" "Oh lovely," I said "I'm going to just puncture that lovely big balloon" "What are you going to puncture it for!" We'd have been shot up in the air - been the first in space!

In Yiddish there is an expression "Oi'll rip you in sieben stickele!" - which means "I'll rip you into seven pieces!" He had seven children, so he must have ripped one big one into

'Sieben Stickele!" and he always used to say "If you don't behave, Oi'll rip you in sieben stickele!"

The Horse

Before we had the car, we always had horses and traps. I remember one horse - it was a big chestnut horse called Prince - my father loved these horses. The trap was much lower down really, because this horse was so big. I don't know how we got into this cart, really, there were so many of us, and we always had a friend with us, and we always had a dog with us. As soon as we got to Bishopston common, the dog would run off, chasing the sheep, and always get us into trouble.

Anyway, coming down one of the hills in the Gower - a very steep hill - well, the man who had harnessed the horse to the trap hadn't done it properly, and we'd have all been killed - we'd have been flung over the precipice. This horse must have realised that something was wrong when he started off - he was loose in the reins, you see, and he could have galloped off, and we'd have all tumbled down. Well, he slid down on his hind legs, and held back that trap and he saved our lives. I remember that our father flung his arms around this horse's neck and hugged him, because he really had saved our lives. There was another family behind in a horse and trap, and they could see what was happening, and they were shouting "Oh my God! They're all going to get killed!" Anyway, they all realised that this horse had saved our lives.

Now, usually on a Sunday, there were three families - the Samuels, the Cohens, and the Kramskys - we all would arrange to meet down at the Gower Coast in our horses and traps. We would unharness the horses and let them graze on top of the grassy slopes, and we would take them down. By Pwlldu there was a roadway going all the way down and fresh water used to come down in a river to meet the sea there, and then we would water the horses and bring them back up to the slopes. Our horse was busy grazing one day - after we'd had all our picnics with all these people - he was a crazy horse, was Captain. It was strange, because our horse would go clippity, cloppity, clippity, cloppity - you couldn't get him to run fast - until he saw another horse in front of him, then he went raving mad! He used to rush like mad because he had to pass this horse - the trap used to sway from side to side - it was very exciting for the children but my mother used to worry herself to death because it was jolly dangerous - the trap swaying - but once he had passed this horse, he didn't care - he'd go clippity, cloppity, clippity, cloppity again - he was a funny horse.

Anyway, this horse was grazing on the lovely slopes overlooking the beach and all of a sudden he heard a female horse neighing in the distance. Up shot his tail and off he ran down this narrow narrow lane - like mad - and people were just coming with their kids along this narrow pathway and here he was looking for this female horse, this mare, and rushing, and everybody was jumping into the hedges, which were absolutely full of blackberries and thorns and things, to get out of the way. Luckily there was a scoutmaster coming up with a troop, and he managed to jump up on the side of the horse, grabbed hold of the mane, and managed to stop him. Goodness knows what would have happened -he'd have gone mad. Anyway, with my father running after the horse and my brother running after my father, and all the men running after my brother - it would have been a lovely story for a film. Anyway they brought this horse back - my father thanked the scoutmaster for all his troubles. It made everyone quite excited, and the scout troop, about this little adventure.

The Police

Sometimes on a Sunday my father used to go and see a customer and we used to bundle into the back of the car, with my mother in front with a baby on her lap (for a change). We went right out into the country, and as we were going along these narrow lanes, the lights fused! It was getting dark and he didn't have his lights on; he was going to a strange place - when, like a light from heaven, a car came behind us with full headlights on. Well, my father - in desperation - kept this car behind us all the way - he wouldn't let him pass. So when we came to a wide part of the road, he could have let him pass by a gateway or somewhere - he was tooting and blowing his horn - so when we got to a wide part, he passed us and he went and reported us to the police that we were going without any lights - he thought we were trying to save battery.

So when we got to the first lot of police, of course - we were looking for a garage, we had to leave the car there for the battery to be charged - when the police, in this little country place, stopped us, my father explained that we were looking for a garage. So they let us go on. By now, we had come to a little bit of gas-lit street, you see. So of course, we'd only gone about a hundred yards; another two policemen stopped us. This was going on and on, so eventually we had come back to try and look for this garage - we had to go to another stretch and then - you know, you can never find a policeman when you want one - but suddenly, all the police. Then we saw another two policemen, and my father said "Oh, to hell with this - I'm not stopping any more!"

So these two policemen must have telephoned through to another two policemen, and by that time—there was this car with all these kids in it, and my father driving, and my mother with a baby on her lap - six police were chasing us, mostly on their bikes. It was like one of those Charlie Chaplin films—in those days they didn't have panda cars - they were all on their bikes chasing us down these narrow lanes - I can't help laughing when I think of it. Of course, we got to a garage and they all came along and charged my father with a summons, my father, for travelling without any lights and also obstructing this other car - keeping him behind us all the time! Anyway, when they heard the story—my mother was crying by this time - with a baby on her lap crying; the kids were all howling because they were hungry and cold and miserable. I think the police were glad to get rid of us really.

14.   Big Trouble (with little rabbits)

TELEPHONE 2754.

J. KRAMSKY, Ltd.
RABBIT SKIN MERCHANTS.

LIMEKILN YARD,
   UPPER STRAND,
      SWANSEA.

Rabbit Skins

Alongside the scrap business, Jack also dealt in rabbit skins. People would shoot the rabbits – a detested pest which ate many farmers' crops - and bring him the skins to be dried, which were then turned into fur coats.

WESTERN MAIL & SOUTH WALES NEWS,
THURSDAY, OCTOBER 23, 1930.

MISCELLANEOUS WANTS

WANTED, 50,000 Rabbit Skins; best market prices paid; large or small quantities; inquiries solicited.—J. Kramsky, Ltd., Limekiln Yard, Upper Strand, Swansea. Tel. 2754.
2

WESTERN MAIL & SOUTH WALES NEWS,
WEDNESDAY, DECEMBER 20, 1939.

MISCELLANEOUS WANTS

QUALITY Rabbit Skins, 4/6d. to 6/- per doz.; Quality Mixed Rags, 10/- to 16/- per cwt.; Woollens, 6d. per lb.; Flannels, 2d. per lb ; Wrapper:. 2/6d. per dozen. Top prices paid for Sacks, Metals. Scrap Iron, Jars and Bottles, &c.—J. Kramsky, Ltd., Upper Strand, SWANSEA. Tel. 2754.

The Western Daily Press
AND BRISTOL MIRROR
BRISTOL, THURSDAY, SEPTEMBER 11, 1941

MISCELLANEOUS WANTS.

5,000 Dozen RABBIT SKINS Wanted weekly. We pay top prices. Inquiries solicited.—J. Kramsky Ltd., Upper Strand, Swansea. Tel. 2754. By Helping Your King and Country You Help Yourself: We pay for SCRAP IRON £3 per ton: Rags 15s cwt. Top prices for Woollens, Stockings, Flannels, Lead, Brass, Copper, Horse Hair, Bags, Feathers, Jam Jars and Bottles.

When war broke out in 1939, Jack managed to get a lucrative contract selling the skins to the US Army, to line their winter coats.

The first consignment of top-grade rabbit skins was lost when the transport ship carrying them across the Atlantic to the USA was sunk. Although some money was recovered from the insurance, it was not enough to cover their cost. So, thinking the second consignment would suffer the same fate, lower quality skins were sent the next time. However - Jack's luck - the ship got through, and that's when the trouble started....

The Case of the Rabbit Skins

My father always kept the scrap business going - that made enough money to keep our family, but on the sidelines there was always a chance of making money. So he used to deal in rabbit skins—people used to go out shooting rabbits, and they would bring in the skins to him to be dried, and then he would send them off to be made into fur coats. I remember them coming into our house sometimes, on a Saturday night, when they were sorted out into first, second and third grades, depending on the type of fur the rabbits had. I can still remember the horrible smell! But we still made a bit of money from that. When war broke out, my father managed to get a contract to sell these furs or rabbit skins to America - they wanted to use them for the Army uniforms - when they sent them to cold climates, to line their coats with. So he commandeered this train in Swansea, and then the boat was to take them over to America. During that time, they were bombing the transport ships going from America to England, or vice-versa. So my father put the best, first-rate skins into this boat - it was to make him a lot of money - and the boat that was taking the skins over was bombed, and sank. My father hadn't insured them for as much as he should have, so he didn't get all that much - not as much as he would have done, but still he had quite a bit.

"So!" he thought to himself. "Well, if the ship is going to get bombed, or torpedoed, the next lot - why should I send the first-rate skins? I'll mix them a little bit - some first, some second, some third! If it gets bombed, they won't know! Then this time I'll insure it for quite a bit of money, and I'll be rich!" But his luck - he should have realised that he wasn't that so lucky in his life - that ship got through. So of course the furriers said "We're not paying you the amount of money we agreed, because you said that you were sending us first class skins, and you've sent us a mixed lot. So we're going to halve it." So my father refused to accept the half, and can you imagine that this case went on for sixteen years? Every time the people fought the case in America, they won; when my father fought the case in England, he won, and this went on for sixteen years! In the meantime, my father was paying all this money to his solicitors to fight his case for him!

So you know now, that my name is Mrs. Siegfried Bachenheimer - I have to say this, because during the time that my husband was in the army, my father said to me "You must go up to London to fight this case, because otherwise the bailiffs will come in and take all your mother's furniture, and all the money will be taken away, and we'll be left without a penny." This was because the rabbit skin case had taken nearly all his money, and they were now trying to sue him for the money, because he was having so many cases. So to try to save money, what he had done was to put money into my account, and to make me the chief creditor. I don't know much about this business, only I was always scared of going to court, because my father was always having his court cases. Not that he was a criminal, but in business it always happens. So I said "I'm not going up to London to fight a case!" "It's nothing," he said. "This solicitor, Mr. Jones, is going to be up there, and he'll do the case, but you've only got to say to the judge that the money is all yours."

I never knew I was so rich! But I only knew that my father had opened a banking account for me, in my name, and said that I was the chief creditor, and the bailiffs, or anybody else, couldn't touch my mother's house - because I owned everything! I was a bit slow there, come to think of it - everything was mine -little did I know what it meant! In name only, you see! Now, I didn't even know what an affidavit was, but I had to go to a solicitor and sign a paper - that was supposed to be swearing an affidavit which was to mean that everything I said was the truth - that's what I assumed it meant. My father had said "All you'll have to do is to go into a little room in the law courts" I didn't even know what the law-courts looked like. So I went to these big law-courts in Holborn—you can imagine! Here was this little me, coming into these big law-courts - I remember I had a little green coat on, with a little astrakhan collar, and a little velvet beret, and no money - only what my father had given me to get up to London to fight this case. My father had said "You'll go into this room, and there'll only be a little man there, and all he'll say to you is 'Is this the truth?' and you'll say 'Yes, sir! Three bags full, sir!' and that's all you'll have to say"

I came into this room - I nearly died! There were quite a lot of people - press people sitting there, and opposite me around this table was a big barrister with a wig on. His name was Levy - I'll always remember that. Here was I - a tiny little thing, and I was supposed to oppose this man. The solicitor didn't say anything, it's true that the little man - the judge - wasn't in a wig, he was sitting there with his little tiny glasses on. Now there comes the cross-examination - can you imagine how I felt?

This is how it began: "You are Mrs. Siegfried Bachenheimer?" "Yes." "You are married to a German refugee, who came here without any money. So tell me, my dear, how have you got all this money in the bank? And how is it that you, an ordinary type of person, has a bank account?" In those days you didn't normally have an account. So I had to think of all these lies and stories to tell him, because I have to think to myself - 'They're going to take everything away from my parents, after all their hard work to bring up us seven children.' - so now my fighting spirit got up, really, but I didn't really know what he was going to say "But you swore an affidavit!" So I kept turning to the little judge and saying "But I don't know what he means, sir!"

All my acting ability - I had done amateur dramatics in my time - really helped me in this; by this time I really could have sat down and howled! I didn't know what was being talked about - my father had never told me anything about it except that I was the chief creditor. Now comes the questions and answers: "If you had a job," - he knew all about me - "in a shop in London, earning about a pound a week, how is it that you were able to save up all this money?" "Well," I said. "I didn't just work in the shop like that, I worked on commission, and I used to have a Saturday job, working in the market; and I used to have a Sunday job, and I earned a lot of money..." - the fibs I was telling!

Now my back was up, and I really had to fight back - everything had to be told, and every time I couldn't answer a question, I turned to the little judge, and I said "I don't know what he means, Sir!" "You have a deposit account here." "I know," I said. "Besides, how do you know my husband was a German refugee? He knows very well that my husband was running away from Hitler, and he had been a very rich man in his time, and before he became a refugee, he had been a stamp collector, and he had some very valuable stamps in the sole of his shoe, and he'd brought them out of the country, and when I met him, he had that amount of money. So he wasn't a poor refugee, because he had this stamp collection which we could sell whenever we wanted to."

He had my bank book there, and I didn't even know how much money I had in it. So he said "How is it that you have such an amount in your account, two lots, put in one week after another?" My father had put it in quick, you see, so that no-one would know who much money he had if he wanted to get out of the business quick! "Well," I said. "When a Jewish girl gets married, she gets a dowry. My father had put money in for a dowry for me, and my mother didn't want my father to know, so she had put some money in as well for a dowry the next week! So that neither of them would know how much I was to have. Not only that, Sir," I said to the judge. "Mr. Levy should know about it, because he's Jewish as well. So he would know it's the truth I'm saying about a dowry, because no doubt it would have happened to him, Sir!"

Oh, this Mr. Levy's looking at me could have killed me by this time. I was choked, and I was thinking that my poor brother Morry was a prisoner of war in Japan, and I'm saying to the judge "I don't know what all this is about, Sir. My husband is fighting in the army, my brother is a prisoner of war in Japan, and I really am so upset by that, and there he is making me out to be a liar, Sir. I feel so upset I can't tell you. I feel I want to sit down and cry." "Well," said the judge. "Can you answer his questions, my dear?" "I don't know what he's talking about," I said. "I've been a Girl Guide, and I don't tell lies. I never tell lies - I don't know why he's making me out to be such a liar. I feel terrible about it, Sir." In the end, the judge summed up like this - my father's solicitor was getting paid for this, and he hadn't said a word! I was choked, really, that this was happening to me. he said to the prosecuting counsel.

"Well, there is no evidence to say that this young lady has not been telling the truth, and as she has explained, a Jewish girl, as you know, does get a dowry, and therefore that's why she's got the money that she says she has in her banking account, and she said she wanted to open a business for her husband when he comes out of the army, and that's why she opened the account. So I don't think there's any evidence to say that she's not been proved innocent."

So I came out of there, and I rushed down the corridors of this huge courts - I can still remember it - every time I pass them I get the shivers. This Mr. Levy slammed the door on me - he was so furious that this little slip of a girl could really win the case against him. The solicitor was standing outside, and said "I congratulate you, Esther." "I don't want you to tell me anything! Leave me alone!"

I'd arranged to meet my sister Leah, and my husband's sister Ruth in Lyon's Corner House - they used to have a tea place and continental brasserie there which served continental food downstairs, and music played. I always remember, as I was coming in the door, my sister was coming down the stairs, and I was coming up, and she said "Well, how did you get on?" and I burst out crying. "Leave me alone! I don't want to talk about it! I feel so bad" "Never mind," she said. "Meet Ruth, and we'll go downstairs, and we'll have a real slap-up meal and a bottle of wine" - on the money my father had given me to get up to London. I had all these pound notes in my hand, and Ruth was reminding me - when I went to South Africa - that we got quite drunk, and the waitress came and said "What are you celebrating?" "I'm celebrating my divorce!" I said, and there was his sister sitting right next to me!

I was so upset, but I did have the money my father had given me for expenses, and he gave me some money in the Post Office when I came back, and he was very grateful. When I look back, I really saved the family honour, because the boys - my brothers - would have come back from the army, and my husband as well; they'd have had no job to go back to - their business would have gone! I was very silly really - I should have cashed in on that. I never took advantage of that, come to think of it!

In August 1943, the London company of "Hide Fur & Skin Brokers Ltd" (their advert is above) petitioned the HIgh Court, requesting that they wind up the company of J Kramsky Ltd, as an amount of £744.12.5 (plus costs) had not been repaid since July 1942. Also mentioned the amount of £500, recently paid to an Esther Bachenheimer.

Receivers were appointed to sell off the entire contents of his yard at Limekiln Yard, at an auction which take place on 18th September 1943.

THE LONDON GAZETTE, 3 SEPTEMBER, 1943

In the High Court of Justice (Chancery Division).
—Companies Court. No. 00229 of 1943.
Mr. Justice Bennett.
In the Matter of J. KRAMSKY Ltd., and in the Matter of the Companies Act, 1929.
NOTICE is hereby given that a petition for the winding-up of the above named Company by the High Court of Justice was on the 6th day of August 1943 presented to the said Court by Hide Fur and Skin Brokers Ltd. whose registered office is situate at Brook's Wharf, 48, Upper Thames Street in the city of London, and that the said petition is directed to be heard before the Court sitting at the Royal Courts of Justice, Strand, London, on the 18th day of October. 1943 and any creditors or contributory of the said Company desiring to support or oppose the making of an Order on the said petition may appear at the time of hearing in person or by his Counsel for that purpose, and a copy of the petition will be furnished to any creditor or contributory of the said Company requiring the same by the undersigned on payment of the regulated charge for the same.

J. KRAMSKY LIMITED

Petition of Hide Fur and Skin Brokers Limited, a Judgment Creditor for £744.12. 5 and £120. 7. 0 costs, for the usual Compulsory Order.

Notice under the Courts (Emergency Powers) (No. 1) Rules 1941 has been served but the Company did not apply for relief.

Execution was issued but the assets were successfully claimed in interpleader proceedings by the Receiver for the holder of a debenture for £500. It is alleged that there is a prior debenture for £100.

The Petition has been duly verified, served and advertised.

In November 1943, the receivers appointed a liquidator who would only be released in May 1950. J Kramsky Limited was finally struck off the company register in 1954.

Meanwhile in March 1944, Jacob Kramsky applied to be discharged from his 1933 personal bankruptcy; this was refused.

SALES BY AUCTION

By ORDER of the DEBENTURE HOLDERS re J. KRAMSKY, LTD. Upper Lime Kiln Yard, The Strand, Swansea.

JNO. OLIVER WATKINS, F.S.I., F.A.I., has received instructions from the Receiver and Manager to OFFER for SALE by TENDER the whole of the Stock, Office Furniture and Motor Cars including 3 Tons Mixed Rags, 5 Tons Linsey, 3 Tons Thirds, 2 Tons Seams, 35cwt Bagging, 3,000 Jam Jars and Bottles, 2 Tons Old Tyres, 4cwt. Inner Tubes, 6cwt. Wool, 30cwt. Seconds, 8 Transformers, Quantity Firewood, 3 Tons Battery Lead, 10cwt. Copper, 21cwt. Mixed Brass, 23cwt. Zinc, 4cwt. Lead, 2 Tons Raffia Matting, 230 Jude Sacks, 2cwt. Feathers, 5cwt. Platform Scale, 10cwt. Platform Scale, 1cwt. Platform Scale, 30in. Saw Bench, 2 Sack Trucks, 2 Wire Screens, 30in. Steel Safe by Withers, Oak Pedestal Writing Desk, Deal Pedestal Writing Desk, 5 Chairs, 4-drawer Foolscap Steel Filing Cabinet, 4-drawer Foolscap Cabinet in oak, 2 Stationery Cupboards, Eight-day Time Clock, Remington Typewriter, 18in. carriage, Writing Bureau Typist's Table, First Aid Outfit, Double Fish and Chip Range, and a Lead Pipe Making Plant (dismantled), and Sundry Book Debts. MOTOR CARS—Singer 8 Van (1935), Morris 8 Saloon (1936) 1 Ton Morris Commercial (1929), together with miscellaneous quantity of Marine Stores. Tenders to be sent by 12 Noon on SEPT. 22 to the Receiver and Manager, Norman S. Webber, Esq., of Messrs. Ronald Cross and Co., Incorporated Accountants Bonvilter., Swansea. Further details of the goods, together with a permit to view to be obtained of Jno. Oliver Watkins, Auctioneer, 28, Walter-road, Swansea.   u168

15. Legal Matters

£75 Fines Under Paper Control Order

J. Kramsky, Ltd., Upper Strand, Swansea, were fined a total of £75 and ordered to pay 10 guineas costs by the local justices on Tuesday for three offences under the Control of Paper Order.

Mr. L. C. Thomas, for the Ministry of Supply, said that the first two summonses concerned the offer to sell linsey garments at prices exceeding the maximum, which was £11 per ton.

Kramsky asked £14 10s. per ton, which was £3 10s. per ton above the maximum. In the third summons the defendant offered to sell a quantity of roofing rags to Messrs. Witter at £11 per ton when the controlled price was £7 10s.

Mr. Thomas said this was an obvious case of holding up essential war material which was wanted for the manufacture of paper.

For the defence Mr. W. R. Francis submitted that the offences were committed in innocence. Both Kramsky's son and manager were in the Forces and Kramsky himself, not being very well educated, did not appreciate the proper meaning of the Regulations.

In 1942, Jack was in trouble again, this time for selling paper and clothes at a price higher than that allowed. After the outbreak of war, rationing had been introduced on many items such as food, petrol and clothes, which also restricted the maximum price that these could be sold for.

16. Up the Strand

Welcombe House, at 91-92 Strand, in the 1960s and in 2016

Strand

While the road names "Strand" and "Upper Strand" are close in name, and just a few minutes' walk away through the foot tunnel beneath Swansea train station, they are miles apart in terms of class and prestige. Upper Strand, north of the station, was part of the rough, lower-class Hafod area of Swansea. Strand is south of the station, and while still just outside the centre, is closer to the Market & the Castle, and closer to the larger shops on the High Street.

Not permitted to be a company director, and having just had the contents of Limekiln Yard sold off at the end of 1943, you may think that would be the end of Jack's business career, however...

In 1944, a new company called Universal Waste Materials Ltd can be found trading at 91-92 Strand.

In 1946, they are advertising for electrical equipment and dynamos.

In 1950, they are fighting a court case regarding waste paper.

On 11th April 1958, Jack Kramsky died.

On 24th October 1958, petitions for winding up both Universal Waste Materials Limited, and F V Blake (Wales) Limited, were presented to the High Courts by the Westminster Bank.

Welcombe House

After Jack died, his sons Isy & Morry changed the business direction, away from scrap & recycling, and into the car business. In 1960 they were involved in the building of a large multi-storey office block on the site, with a car showroom on the ground floor.

Welcombe House Motors Ltd was a Swansea landmark here throughout the 1960s, selling many brands of British cars, and running an Esso petrol station on the side, until they ceased trading in 1970.

The Ministry of Transport then took over the building, housing the Vehicle Inspectorate, which became the Vehicle and Operator Services Agency (VOSA). They finally moved out in 2008, and as of 2019 the building stands empty.

Kieft Cars

KIEFT

Holder of 13 World Records
in Classes and J

500 c.c. Car, complete with Speedway J.A.P. engine, £585
Features include Light Alloy Chassis and Wheels, Rubber
Suspension, T. L. S. Brakes.

KIEFT CARS LTD., TRADING ESTATE, BRIDGEND.

Cyril Kieft, born in Swansea in 1911, designed Formula 3 racing cars, using 500cc motorcycle engines, in the early 1950s. These were built by his company in Langland Bay, and tested at Fairwood Aerodrome, later moving to works in Bridgend.

Stirling Moss and other drivers won many Formula 3 races in Kieft cars, and Don Parker won the 1952 championship in one. A road car was planned but never built; the factory moved and the company changed ownership.

Kieft machinery was displayed & sold at the Welcombe House showroom in the Strand, though it is not known how profitable this was!

16/end

17. And so to Bishopston

Sheila & Rita on the gate of Sunrise

Sunrise & Shalom

One summer in 1946, as the Kramsky family were spending the summer in Ridley Way in Bishopston, conversation turned to the subject of some new houses that they could see being built on the other side of the field behind their cottage.

As it turned out, the new owners were to be Mrs B Kramsky, and Mrs E Blake, who were constructing a pair of semi-detached houses on Gerret's Hill, on the Bishopston Road. Esther deposited an initial £20 for the plot of land on 12th May 1945, just four days after the end of the war, followed by £226 ten days later. Payments to builders "Dyke & Greenwood" of Pyle Corner were in instalments; £150 each from Mrs Kramsky & Mrs Blake in January 1946, the same again in May, and a final £384 in October.

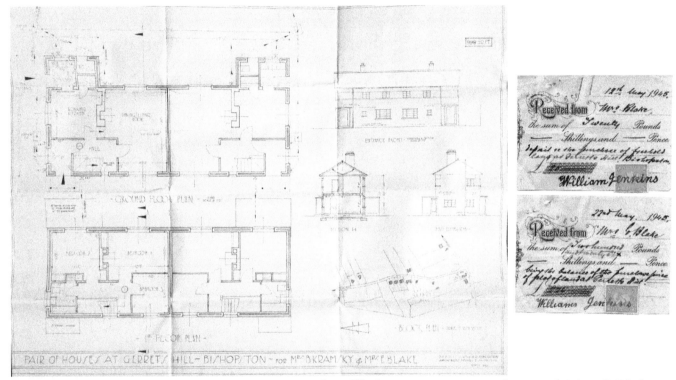

Plans for "A pair of houses at Gerret's Hill, for Mrs B Kramsky, and Mrs E Blake

On one side, Jack & Betty would live in "Shalom" for the rest of their lives. From 1952-60, the phone number (in the name of B Kramsky) was Bishopston 3196, changing to 396 from 1961-68.

On the other side, Esther & Freddie would live in "Sunrise" until 1954, with their children Rita, Sheila and Alan, all attending Bishopston School. Their phone number was Bishopston 196, in the name of F V Blake, from 1951-54.

Having no need of fences, they shared the gardens; as well as sharing it with various egg-laying fowl, and fruit & vegetable patches.

Freddie Blake

Freddie had been born in Braunschweig in 1915, as Seigfried Bachenheimer. Initially training as a dental mechanic, he emigrated in 1937 to Sweden, after the rise of Hitler, where he worked on a farm which bred horses. In August 1939, he made it to England, just 10 days before the outbreak of war, and worked on a dairy farm, before joining the 88th Company.

Sent to France as part of the British Expeditionary Force, and evacuated from St Malo in 1940, he was stationed all over England and Wales, including a spell at the Caswell Bay Hotel in Mumbles. Playing violin in the company band on his days off, practicing tenor saxophone, and meeting the Jewish girls at the TOC-H, he ran into Leah Kramsky, who was visiting her sister in hospital. The sister was Esther, and they kept in touch...

Esther and Freddie married in Wales on 23rd September 1942. Under the "Aliens Act", Esther automatically became a German citizen. Although she was granted "re-admission" just a few months later, Freddie had to wait until the end of the war to apply. Their certificates of naturalisation show –

Bachenheimer, Esther; Germany; Omnibus Conductress; Ridley Way, Caswell Corner, Bishopston, Swansea, S Wales. 12 February, 1943.

Blake, Fred Vernon (formerly Siegfried Bachenheimer); Germany; Dental Mechanic; "Inglenook," Bishopston, Swansea, S Wales. 6 December, 1946.

Posted to Ashford, he helped to get the troops dentally fit for D-Day. After being demobbed, he was back in Swansea, where Rita had been born the previous September. First he set up as a dental mechanic in Swansea, but only for a few months. Next he worked for his father-in-law; "not a happy situation". When Isy came back from Italy, and Morry from Japan, the sons both went to work for their father, so Freddie was "given another place to work in Llanelli".

F V Blake Wales Ltd (Metal Merchants) is listed at Princess Street, Llanelly for 1951-53, and then at Sidings, Burry Port in 1954. The plan was then to move to Birmingham where Morry was also in the scrap metal business; however a change of heart saw the family moving to Ilford in 1954, selling Sunrise for £2390. There he founded Fred Blake (Tools) Ltd, distributors of tools and accessories to the trade in Plaistow, London, which he ran until his death in 1992.

Most of the Kramskys at the wedding of Esther & Fred Blake in 1942

Betty's Travels

Betty began to travel further afield later in life; in 1948 she obtained a British passport. She travelled either alone or with a friend, to visit children and relatives, as well as to see the sights.

In 1948 she travelled to Switzerland & France, in 1949 Italy, in 1950 France and Germany, in 1951 Germany, in 1954 France, in 1957 Haifa by ship from Marseilles, and in 1958 and 1960 she travelled by ship to New York.

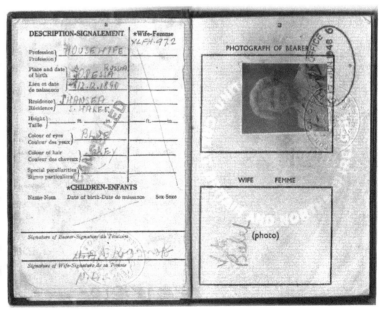

Bishopston Road in 1956

Dylan Thomas (again)

In 1937 David John Thomas retired from teaching at Swansea Grammar School, and moved from the famous house in Cwmdonkin Drive, with his wife Florence, to 133 Bishopston Road. Dylan often stayed there with his parents, picnicking on Caswell Bay, and writing poems such as "Ballad Of The Long-Legged Bait" there, in 1941.

> [..]
>
> Good-bye, good luck, struck the sun and the moon,
>
> To the fisherman lost on the land.
>
> He stands alone at the door of his home,
>
> With his long-legged heart in his hand

The house is directly opposite 154/156; the present owners of 154 often see tourists taking photos of the house opposite. Although Thomas' parents moved to Blaencwm in about 1943, they surely would have met in Bishopston village, while the Kramskys were staying in their cottage in Ridley Way.

Chirpy

[Esther]

My mother and us both kept a lot of chickens. We had a very broody hen, who was sitting on these eggs for such a long time and one day we went out there and saw she'd squashed a couple, and so we took the one remaining whole egg, took it away from the stupid mother hen, and put it in a basket with cotton wool. We put it in at the bottom of this oven, which was very very warm. So early in the morning my sister and I came in and we saw this little basket, which wasn't being cooked - it was just nicely warm, and there we heard a pecking and pecking and we thought 'Oh dear, this chick must be trying to come out of the egg'.

Anyway all of a sudden we saw this little beak coming out so we started helping it. Actually it comes out by itself but we thought we'd give it a hand - we pulled a bit of the shell off and there was this little chick come out. It looked so terrible, it was all wet and horrible and it had like a little crown like Jesus - a little white piece of shell it was. So we took it outside - the sun was shining - and we put it on the grass. In ten minutes or less it fluffed up into the most beautiful yellow fluffy chick - you can't believe it. So anyway we christened it Chirpy and it's a miracle but it started pecking right away at the grass - it doesn't have to be taught - better than human beings really - it was self-sufficient immediately. But it thought that I was the mother because it cottons onto the first thing it sees, so of course it chased me all round the place and "squeea!" all the time "squeea! squeea! squeea! squeea! squeea!" I couldn't even go to the toilet - followed me in. Anyway we went upstairs and went to bed that night and in the middle of the night - it was worse than having a baby in the house - it was at the bottom of the stairs crying.

So my husband had to come downstairs, put the little chick in his hand and it lay its head right down on his fist and went to sleep - it wanted the warmth you see. Well, he never stayed up all night with the babies, but he stayed up all night with the chick and of course it followed us about everywhere - followed the three children about, because it thought well, they were its brothers and sisters. It didn't know that it was a chicken - thought it was a human being, just that we didn't really have to feed him much.

That chick grew up and it became like a watchdog - nobody was allowed to come near that house. It became a beautiful cockerel - the colours on that were fantastic; but when we came to London we had to leave it behind- we were heartbroken to leave him there - he was just like one of the family. I often think about little Chirpy.

Rita & Sheila with their grandparents, in Bishopston

Swansea Synagogue

JACOB KRAMSKY. לב ניסן ‏יעקב ב"ר שלום

BETTY KRAMSKY ו' תשרי ‏ביזא בת ר' ישראל

A Seder at Swansea Synagogue, c1950. Jack is seated, second from left.

PRESENTED BY
MR & MRS. KRAMSKY
SWANSEA
1956 —— 5 716.

This mantel covers the Torah scroll which is used for Shabbat services. The congregation is now very small, and attendance modest, so these services are held only around once a month.

End of an Era

Jack passed away on 11th April 1958; on that day, the top selling record in the UK pop charts was "Magic Moments" by Perry Como.

When Betty died on 28th September 1968, the record at number one was "Those Were The Days" by Mary Hopkin; an English translation of a Russian song recorded in 1926 by Alexander Vertinsky. Vertinsky was born in Kiev, Ukraine, but left for Europe in the early 1920s. Coincidentally, Jack's cousin Rosa Kramsky married a Leon Vertinsky who later emigrated to Israel.

Looking Back

In September 2016, Rita & Sheila visited number 154, and met the current owners, Glynis & Brian, who have lived there since 1993. In the intervening decades, the house has been extended, the formerly joint 154/156 garden divided, and the chicken coops long gone. Bishopston Road is wider now, with considerably more traffic; no more running after cars to write down their number plates. Horses no longer wander down from the common to graze in the front garden, and Withy Farm was long ago developed into a road full of new houses. In Bishopston though, some things change but slowly; Vernon Hughes, now nearly 90, still lives next door at number 152, and remembers Jack, Betty, Annie, and especially Leah. The edible nasturtiums are still in the front garden; and despite much overpainting, the old mezuzahs inside number 154 are still attached to their door posts.

18. Disaster in Swansea

THE DAILY MAIL

WEATHER: Fair and mainly bright. LIGHTING-UP: 8.33pm to 6.37am. MOON: Rises 6.24am, sets 6.32pm. RADIO: In Page Four

No. 20,218   TEL. 15100 (15 Lines)   HULL, SATURDAY, SEPTEMBER 9, 1950   Registered for transmission as a Newspaper.

SIX PERISH AS THREE HOUSES COLLAPSE

Children Burned in Debris

A 74-YEAR-OLD MAN and five children were killed and 15 other people taken to hospital when three houses in Prince of Wales-rd., Swansea, crashed to the ground in a pile of rubble early today. Of those taken to hospital, 10 are seriously injured.

Rescue workers, some still wearing their pyjamas, were watched by crowds as they worked among the ruins to release two other people believed to be trapped. The man who was killed was Samuel H. Belkin. He was rushed to hospital when extricated from the debris, but was dead on arrival at the hospital. The five children are so far unidentified.

Adjoining houses were affected by the crash, and their occupants were told to find alternative accommodation, as the houses are thought to be in a dangerous condition.

The houses fell into a nearby yard and left a huge gap in the street.

Neighbours who were awakened between 6am and 6.30am by the noise of the falling houses rushed to the scene. Rescue work continued throughout the morning, watched by hundreds of people.

ROARING NOISE

One neighbour, Mr F. Sweeting, said, "I was awakened this morning by a terrific roaring and rushing noise. On going to my bedroom window I saw a great pall of dust going up from the ruins. The fall left a huge gap in the street where the houses had been."

Three women, after getting out of the debris, went to neighbours' houses before they were sent to hospital.

It is believed that before the houses crashed, some stables and garages which are underneath the houses had fallen.

After a little time, continued Mr Lewis, he heard men shouting above him and asking if there was anyone there.

"I put my hand up through the debris and shouted, 'Yes, can you see my hand.'

"They shouted back that they could not see it and then I got hold of a stick, pushed it up through the debris and they saw it."

Rescuers working feverishly in the ruins of the collapsed house in Prince of Wales-rd., Swansea, in an effort to release the people buried under the debris. Hull Daily Mail picture by portable transmitter from Swansea.

News of the disaster made headlines in Wales, England, and Australia

First Collapse in 1914

The row of houses had been built in the 1890s, when planning laws were none too strict, on a huge retaining wall built alongside the Strand, nearly 60-80 feet high. Due to the steepness of the hillside, and the strength of the wall, the houses were subject to periodic slips; in 1914 neighbouring houses 21-23 had collapsed and destroyed part of that wall, taking 100 tons of earth down with them.

Cambria Daily Leader

THE PIONEER OF THE — WELSH DAILY PRESS.

No. 12,785. (First Issued 1861) SWANSEA, THURSDAY, MAR. 12, 1914. [Registered at the General Post Office as a Newspaper.] ONE HALFPENNY.

ANOTHER LANDSLIDE.

PRECARIOUS CONDITION OF SWANSEA COTTAGES.

COLLAPSE OF WALL.

The position in Prince of Wales-road, Swansea, and down below it, in Flint-mill-row, where the serious subsidence took place on Tuesday afternoon, is still extremely critical and dangerous.

At about 3.30 this morning there was yet another considerable fall, a full length of brick wall which separates the backyards of No. 17 and 18, Prince of Wales-road, giving way, and tumbling below with a tremendous crash.

No. 17 is occupied by Mrs. Baddiel, a widow, who keeps a general shop. The next house is occupied by Mrs. Kalpus, whose husband is a traveller. An examination of the backyard this morning revealed a very dangerous state of things. A portion of the dividing brick wall hung sheer, and a square bricked corner, which is cracked, seemed to have very little support. Mrs. Kalpus has removed some chickens from there in fear of a fall.

Ceiling Cracked.

Across the kitchen of No. 17, Mrs. Baddiel showed our representative a long crack extending right across the ceiling, which she first noticed this morning.

Mrs. Baddiel, Mrs. Kalpus, and others were standing out in their back yards, close against the wall when the first fall occurred on Tuesday, and it was only by a movement that Mrs. Baddiel was saved from falling with it.

Roar Like Thunder.

The "Leader" man went down to Flint Mill-row, and found a considerable family still living in one of the damaged houses. They were in the front room, which contained a large bed. He had a chat with Mrs. Harris, wife of Mr. John Harris, the tenant, who is a dock labourer.

She told how she was aroused this morning by a roar like thunder, when the second crash came. She also stated that two other families were living in the doomed cottages next door—one a Hafod employe with five children, another a dock labourer, with three children.

Our representative came away with the conviction that if appalling results are to be avoided—fortunately, up to the moment, there has been no damage to life or limb—two things are urgently demanded to be done, and that without the loss of a moment; first, to provide reasonable shelter for these three distracted families; and second, to begin the work of shoring up the bank.

In 1914, the land-slip happened at around 4pm on a Tuesday afternoon, when fortunately not many people were home, otherwise lives would have been lost. The retaining wall was repaired, but remained a "disaster waiting to happen."

Collapse in 1950

In the early hours of Saturday 9th September 1950, three houses on the Prince of Wales Road collapsed backwards into the Strand below, killing seven people and injuring fifteen, some seriously. Two days later, two more houses collapsed, and two weeks later another three partly collapsed; fortunately they had already been evacuated after the first collapse.

After the 1950 collapses, a survey found that the remaining houses were leaning 6 inches towards the Strand, and that in some cases the floors were 11 inches lower at the back of the house than the front.

An inquest returned a verdict of accidental death, and exonerated the owners from blame; the collapsed houses were owned by 5 separate people, including the "Kramsky sisters of Bishopston."

The houses were never rebuilt, and remained in their wrecked condition, until 1965, when that part of Prince of Wales Road was flattened and the arches filled in, to make way for the New Cut Road.

Kramsky blamed

[Esther]

As they got near to the Strand, there was a terrible commotion, and they would have lynched my father - they put the blame on him. I don't know why they were blaming my father - the houses just happened to be his. So he got blamed - it wasn't just that he lost the property - and he lost a lot of money for it. We were very very unhappy to think that Shm'chayim and these four children had been killed - it was not our fault, but we had to take Dad back to the bungalow because he was a Jew, and the other non-Jews blamed my Dad. They found out afterwards that it had been a gas explosion—it was nobody's fault. But what had happened was all these houses had caved in and they'd gone right down into the valley - a very very sad time that was - whatever it was.

The strange part about it - some of those houses at the top of that street would have tumbled down years ago, because there was a lot of land subsidence, and they propped the houses at the top of the hill - built them up again - some of those houses are still standing.

But the other row of houses that we were in as children - there's nothing left of that - there are all boards there. It's strange - that was the road that used to have the tram-lines going through it - and we weren't quite sure that these houses would withstand the vibrations - every time the tram used to pass the houses used to shake.

19.   The next generation(s)

Isy, Morry, Frances & Leah during the 1939-1945 war.

Sarah, Esther &
Isy, c1917

Sarah, Esther,
Annie & Morry,
c1923

Esther & Sarah,
c1924

Sarah & Leah,
c1927

Jack & Betty had seven children; the wanderlust that had brought them from Russia to Wales, and brought his parents from Poland to America (via Odessa and Wales), continued into the next generation and beyond.

The Boys

Israel Leber Kramsky—Isy Ramsey (aka Edward, Louis) [1912-1997]

Somewhat In the mould of his father, Isy's exploits could fill another book! He "owned" a coal mine, landed an aeroplane in Swansea High Street, blinded himself (temporarily thankfully) defusing unexploded bombs, had pockets full of onions, and a shed full of his "artworks" - sculptures, carvings & paintings.

A family legend has him organising a concert tour for the great American singer Paul Robeson. Robeson certainly sang in Swansea in 1933 & 1937, and at the Pavilion in Mountain Ash in 1938, where he was guest of honour at the memorial to honour the 33 local men who died fighting Fascism during the Spanish Civil War.

Isy is quoted as having been a "miner, steelworker, and fireman", and based on his other professions, who are we to argue?

In 1943, he was an early member of the Jewish Relief Unit; a volunteer group based in London which provided help to refugees and Holocaust survivors. After the war, he was helping refugees in North East Italy, and was involved with the JDC (Joint Distribution Committee) until about 1948.

While working with the JDC in Austria in 1945, he met and married Elfriede (Elfie) Steiner in Vienna. They married at the Seitenstetten-Tempel Synagogue – as her mother was Jewish, Elfriede was "officially" Jewish too. However, Elfriede had been raised as a Catholic, and remained so for the rest of her life.

The Ramsey brothers also found time to run a car showroom, though it may have been more Isy's business with Morry doing the accounts from Birmingham. As a magazine from 1960 has it—

Motor Magazine, 6th July 1960

"What are believed to be the largest car showrooms in Wales, and one of the largest in the United Kingdom are now nearing completion in Swansea for Welcombe House Motors, Ltd., at 91-92 Strand".

The showroom ran successfully for a decade, selling Rovers and other British cars; but was closed in around 1970, when it was taken over by the Ministry of Transport. The building, which stands on the west side of the Park Tawe Retail Park, has been derelict for the past few years, and seems likely to be knocked down and redeveloped.

Welcombe House also displayed & sold Kieft Formula 3 cars; a company which was founded by Swansea-born Cyril Kieft, and whose cars were raced by such drivers as Peter Collins & Stirling Moss.

Isy stayed in the motor trade, opening a car showroom in York Street / Victoria Road, which he ran until the 1980s. He is also remembered for travelling around the country with silver bars in the back of his van. He retired to The Glebe, Bishopston, where he had lived with Elfie since 1948, and devoted himself full time to his painting, sculptures and "gardening".

Morris Kramsky—Morry Ramsey (aka Maurice, Morice) [1920-2005]

Morry had joined the army after the outbreak of war, and been given an administrative post in Belfast, in the cartography department, before volunteering to join the SBS (Special Boat Service, naval equivalent of the RAF's SAS). He was captured in Japan, where he was held as prisoner of war from 1943-1945, listed as "Lance-Corporal Morice Kramskey".

After the war, both Isy & Morry were in Swansea, running both the scrap yards in Upper Strand and Strand with their father.

After a stint working for the Milk Marketing Board, he did very well out of pallets in Birmingham, in a business he ran with Monty Starr.

Morry married Margaret Watling in 1947 in Surrey, and had two children (Michael & Marion), in Swansea, and a third (Grahame) in Birmingham. The family had moved to Birmingham in around 1954, where Morry developed his own successful scrap metal business.

The family soon moved to the Mill House, near Stratford on Avon, where they brought up their children, whose families now live in England, Wales and Hong Kong.

Morry and his sister Esther, with his house, horse & car.

The Girls

Sarah Kramsky (Kantor) [1914-1996]

Sarah appears to have emigrated to Palestine in April 1934, and returned home 6 months later. She married Eddie Kantor, and had a son (Jeffrey) in Essex in 1938. The family emigrated to Australia, where Jeffrey, his wife and his daughters still live.

Esther Kramsky (Bachenheimer aka Blake) [1916-1999]

Esther moved to London during the war, then back to Bishopston where she worked as a clippie on the buses. She married a German soldier (in the British army) Siegfried Bachenheimer, aka Freddie Blake, in 1942, and temporarily became Esther Bachenheimer (Germany spy!). The family—Rita, Sheila & Alan—left Wales in 1954 for Ilford, Essex. They nearly moved to Australia, but changed their mind at the last minute. Children currently living in England & Israel; grandchildren in England, Israel & USA.

Shendale Ann "Annie" Kramsky (Cohen) [1918-1998]

Annie stayed with her parents in Bishopston until a later age, then married (and divorced) a mysterious Mr Cohen, after which she lived in Swansea with a little dog.

Frances Kramsky [1921-2004]

Frances also worked full time for the JCRA (Jewish Committee for Relief Abroad) and JRU (Jewish Relief Unit), in Paris, from 1947 until around 1960. She helped organise and was on board a ship which took more than 900 Jewish refugees from Shanghai, via South Africa, and Naples, to Israel; a journey of some six weeks.

The "Shanghai Ghetto", although in China, had been under Imperial Japanese control since 1937, and was one of the few places which allowed in refugees without passports or visas. By 1943, it was home to over 23,000 Jews. Although conditions were dire and food scarce, the Japanese governor made sure they were not handed over to the Nazis. After liberation in August 1945, Israel and the USA were the most popular destinations; the vast majority had left by 1950.

Frances later travelled around the world; to India, South Africa, Australia. She lived in Paris for many years, drove a succession of sports cars, and ended her days in Biarritz, which reminded her of the Gower coast.

Leah Kramsky (Guiles) [1925-2005]

Leah, the youngest of the seven, was also involved in much charity work, with the Jewish Relief in Italy & Austria in 1945, as well as the Red Cross.

She emigrated to New York in 1952, where she married Don Guiles.

Esther & Isy at the Townhill Jewish Cemetery, Swansea

20. The Americans

Jack was Solomon and Bashi's eldest son, born in 1886. There is a gap of 9 years before their next seven children appear. They all emigrated to the USA; Minnie and Rachel in 1913, and the rest in 1921, along with their parents.

Minnie (1895-1960) – born in Odessa

married Sam (Friedman), had 3 daughters, Beatrice (Kleinman), Gertrude 'Nettie' (Berman), and Goldie (Cohen)

Rachel (1899-1965) – born in Odessa

married William (Bernstecker), had 2 daughters, Sybil (Brown) and Sandra (Friedman)

Lena (1901-1980) – born in Odessa

married Lou (Panich) & ? (Ignatoff), had 1 son, Roy Ignatoff

Rita (1902-1991) – born in Odessa

married Eddie (Karp), 1 daughter, Sheila Karp

Abraham (1904-1977) – born in Odessa

married Lillian (Feintuch), had 3 children, Florrie (Leader), and twins Kenny and Arlene (Halfon)

Beatrice (1907-1960) – born in Wales

married Sol (Schechter), had 1 daughter, Rhoda (Bell)

Sam (1909-1973) – born in Wales

married Betty (Suchin). Their son Melvin married Diane (Wert) and they had two sons, Glenn & Les Kramsky.

Sam was an entertainer, and recorded music under the name of "Ted Kaye"

Photos tbc.

21. Others

There are other Kramskys, documented and undocumented, related and unrelated. This is of necessity an incomplete list, full of rumours & legends.

Solomon's brother Lev.

Lev didn't make it out of the Pale, dying perhaps 1930 in Moldova. His family did emigrate to Palestine; their daughter Rosa marrying Leon Vertinsky in Galilee, son Motiya dying in Ashdod, and son Shimon moving from Tel Aviv to France.

Sam Kramsky

Jack's cousin. Fought in the Spanish Civil War. Emigrated to Palestine and to Mexico. Changed his name to "Levison" after a friend who died in the civil war. Had a daughter called Annette, a stepson called Andre, and an aunt called Molke. Andre visited the family in Wales in the 1950s, and there is a film of him balancing a newly-hatched chick on his head.

Rose Kramsky

Jack's cousin. Second wife of Joseph Langmann, whose son by his first wife Alicheva, Isaac Langmann, married Suzanne. Isaac & Suzanne's daughter Claudie married Michel Akerman, in Paris; their sons are Samuel & David Akerman.

Valli ?

married Moshe Tarragano, in Israel.

Cantor Serotta

Jack's cousin. Apparently a famous singer in the USA.

? Fuks

Betty's sister's family - Argentina?

22.   The Future

In 2019, the Kramsky name is still alive and well, in the families of Gary Kramsky (son of Kenny), and Glenn & Les Kramsky (sons of Melvin).

If we include the "Ramsey" cousins, then we have Michael, Marion and Grahame and their respective sons & daughters.

L'Chaim L'Kramsky!

23. Bibliography & Acknowledgements

The following sources have been used or referred to -

Books—"Mervyn's Lot" by Mervyn Matthews; "Pineapple Sundays" by Haydn Williams; "Down the Memory Lanes of My Hafod" by J Ramsay Kilpatrick; "My Greenhill Far Away" by Brian Ahearne; The Hafod 1920s-1950s by The Hafod History Society; "The Jews of South Wales" by Cai Parry-Jones. "Straight from the Force's Mouth" by David Prowse; "Bleak House" by Charles Dickens.

Manuscript – "Sioma l'Insoumis" by Alexandre Thabor

Periodicals & Directories—London Gazette, Bennetts, Trades, Cope, Kelly's.

Magazines—"Bulgars Britons and Bombers" from "Vault Magazine"

Newspapers—Aberdare Leader, Evening Express, Weekly Mail, Cardiff Times, Merthyr Express, Cambria Leader, South Western Post, Daily Mail, Jewish Chronicle.

Archives—National Archives at Kew; Family History Centre at West Glamorgan Archives

Thanks also to the many family members who have contributed memories, articles & photographs, and to those who have helped with the research, including Gerald Gabb, Bernard Blain & Leonard Mars.

Esther's stories in blue, as told in 1988— available as "The Book of Esther".

Street Views are courtesy of Google, for non-commercial use.

Jacob Kramsky